Fortress • 46

Castles and Tower Houses of the Scottish Clans 1450–1650

Stuart Reid • Illustrated by Graham Turner

Series editors Marcus Cowper and Nikolai Bogdanovic

First published in 2006 by Osprey Publishing
Midland House, West Way, Botley, Oxford OX2 0PH, UK
443 Park Avenue South, New York, NY 10016, USA
E-mail: info@ospreypublishing.com

ISBN 1 84176 962 2

Cartography: Map Studio, Romsey, UK
Design: Ken Vail Graphic Design, Cambridge, UK
Index by Glyn Sutcliffe
Originated by United Graphic, Singapore
Printed and bound in China through Bookbuilders

06 07 08 09 10   10 9 8 7 6 5 4 3 2 1

A CIP catalogue record for this book is available from the British Library.

FOR A CATALOGUE OF ALL BOOKS PUBLISHED BY OSPREY MILITARY AND AVIATION
PLEASE CONTACT:

Osprey Direct, c/o Random House Distribution Center, 400 Hahn Road, Westminster,
MD 21157
Email: info@ospreydirect.com

Osprey Direct UK, P.O. Box 140, Wellingborough, Northants, NN8 2FA, UK
E-mail: info@ospreydirect.co.uk

www.ospreypublishing.com

Author's note

North American readers are advised that British convention is
followed throughout in the naming of floors: the lowest, at ground
level, is the ground floor, while the next is the first floor, and so
on upwards. Basements are always at least partially below ground
level.
For the sake of consistency and for the avoidance of confusion,
reference is made in the text to historical Scottish shires and
counties rather than to post-1974 local government areas. Thus
Bothwell Castle is located in Lanarkshire rather than Strathclyde,
and Edzell Castle stands in Forfarshire rather than Tayside.
In any reference to costing it should be borne in mind that One
Pound Sterling (£1) was equal to Twelve Pounds (£12) Scots.

Artist's note

Readers may care to note that the original paintings from which
the colour plates in this book were prepared are available for
private sale. All reproduction copyright whatsoever is retained by
the Publishers. All enquiries should be addressed to:

Graham Turner
PO Box 568,
Aylesbury
HP17 8ZX,
UK

The Publishers regret that they can enter into no correspondence
upon this matter.

Measurements

Distances, ranges, and dimensions are mostly given in Imperial
measures. To convert these figures to metric, the following
conversion formulae are provided:

1 inch	2.54cm
1 foot	0.3048m
1 yard	0.9144m
1 mile	1.609km
1 pound	0.4536kg

The Fortress Study Group (FSG)

The object of the FSG is to advance the education of the public in
the study of all aspects of fortifications and their armaments,
especially works constructed to mount or resist artillery. The FSG
holds an annual conference in September over a long weekend
with visits and evening lectures, an annual tour abroad lasting
about eight days, and an annual Members' Day.
The FSG journal FORT is published annually, and its newsletter
Casemate is published three times a year. Membership is
international. For further details, please contact:
The Secretary, c/o 6 Lanark Place, London W9 1BS, UK

FRONT COVER
Castle Stalker, in Loch Laich, built c.1495 and recently
restored. (Image: www.undiscoveredscotland.co.uk)

Contents

Introduction

At first sight the great profusion of castles still studding Scotland's landscape seems to underscore the romantic view of its tumultuous and anarchic past created by writers such as Sir Walter Scott and Nigel Tranter. However, a closer look at them reveals a much more complex picture of Scotland's history – and demonstrates how its castles and tower houses were nearly always smaller and very different to their counterparts erected south of the border.

These constructions were shaped both by history and society and in particular by the disastrous Wars of Independence at the outset of the 14th century. Outwardly that conflict was straightforward enough: on a dark and stormy night in 1286 King Alexander III tumbled over a cliff, broke his neck and left no obvious heir. Consequently the various claimants or 'Competitors', 13 in number, submitted their candidacy to Edward I of England for arbitration and while judging the case honestly in favour of John Balliol, he took the opportunity to declare himself Scotland's feudal overlord. The Scots were unimpressed, repudiated his pretensions and after nearly 20 years Robert I – The Bruce – eventually settled the matter at Bannockburn in 1314. To get there,

The tower house at its most bizarre – Amisfield Tower, Dumfriesshire, built in 1628 very much as a 'romantick' castle rather than a serious fortification. Reconstruction by McGibbon and Ross.

however, he first had to fight and win a vicious civil war against the supporters of the Balliols, chiefly led by the Comyns (or Cummings) and the MacDougalls.

Their lands, as it happened, collectively stretched in a great arc from Lorne in the west through Moray and Badenoch to the Buchan coast in the North-East, and included most of what would later become considered as the Highlands. At the time no such distinction existed, but the eclipse of the Comyn lords of Lochaber and Badenoch effectively disenfranchised the Highlands in a Scotland dominated thereafter by the Bruces and their Stewart successors. In the ordinary way of things, the Comyns should simply have been replaced by Bruce allies; and indeed one of his favourite lieutenants, Thomas Randolph, was awarded the Earldom of Moray. However the Randolph line died out within two generations, as did the Bruces themselves, leaving just the Stewarts and the Douglases. Although the former gained and held the Crown long beyond any reasonable expectation, as a family they rapidly declined in importance, as did the Douglases, ravaged by fighting both amongst themselves and with the Stewarts. It is a complicated story, but the upshot was that by the middle of the 15th century the territorial earldoms had effectively collapsed and the 'new' lords who came to prominence did so through Crown patronage and sometimes transient political influence rather than as a reflection of their comparatively modest landholding.

This in turn meant that they had in effect to recruit followers, often through the medium of mutual Bands or Bonds of Man-rent, rather than relying upon their own tenants alone, in order to achieve and maintain that influence. The precise form of these bands varied but essentially they were a contract whereby one gentleman (it was very rare for anyone below the rank of laird to make such a band) pledged his allegiance and that of his kin, friends and servants to another, usually a lord or earl, promising to 'ride and gang' and to assist the lord 'in his actions causes and quarrels' in return for a promise of protection and favour. The Earls of Huntly for example received no fewer than 90 bands, of which nine were made by lords, 71 by lairds, seven by captains of clans, two more generally by a clan, and one by the burgh of Aberdeen. The references in these bands to kin and friends were important, for notwithstanding the feudal veneer, Scotland throughout this period remained very much a clan-based society – one in which John Grant of Freuchie would feel obliged in 1590 to take up the case of two murdered men named Grant, for they were assumed to be his kin or 'at the leist being ane of his surename.' Thus, as King James VI famously complained, men reacted to 'anie displeasure, that they apprehend to be done unto them by their neighbours, to tak up a plaine feid against him and (without respect to God, King or commonweale) to bang it out braifly, hee and all his kinne, against him and all his.'

Predictably enough, although the bands could sometimes have a stabilising influence, generally speaking they resulted in a fragmentation of authority, encouraged feuding, and so led to a certain endemic degree of instability. All of which led a French envoy to report in 1546 that 'The Kingdom of Scotland was, and still is at the present time, under arms; for all the friends of one faction mistrust all those of the other faction; insomuch that not only the nobles are in arms, but churchmen, friars, and peasants travel through the country only in large companies, and all armed with jacks, swords, bucklers, and a half-pike in hand (which they call in this country a lance).'

At the time Scotland was trembling on the brink of the Reformation, and when it came it only made matters worse. As quickly as the vast landholdings of the Catholic church were seized by the Crown, they were parcelled out again amongst great numbers of small proprietors, each of whom if possessed of lands valued at more than £100 Scots per annum was required to erect a 'tour of fence' as a condition of the royal grant. The intention was to assist in the maintenance of law and order by planting what were in effect to be local police stations, which would inhibit the operations of those 'large companies', marauding clansmen, moss-troopers and other outlaw gangs. The fact that these tower houses were mainly to be found in the Lowlands rather than in the Highlands was a simple reflection of the limitations of the Crown's authority in those areas and while they might indeed have served to bridle some of the more blatant lawlessness, inevitably enough they also succeeded in fragmenting authority even further and justified royal edicts such as this one from 1535, which announced:

> It is statute and ordained for saving of men, their goods and gear upon the borders in time of war and of other troublous time, that every landed man dwelling in the inland or upon the borders having there a hundred pound land of new extent shall build a sufficient barmkin upon his heritage and lands in place most convenient of stone and lime, containing 3 score feet (60ft) of the square, an ell (one metre) thick and 6 ells high for the resset and of him his tenants and their goods in troublous time; with a tower in the same for himself if he thinks it expedient. And that all other landed men of smaller rent and revenue build peels and great strengths as they please for saving of themselves men tenants and goods. And that the said strengths barmkins and peels be built and completed within two years under the pain.

At first reading the edict suggests that the towers would have been an innovation, but they were far from it. In a time of religious upheaval and weak royal government, exacerbated by the long regencies which preceded and followed Mary's reign in the second half of the 16th century, a man's home quite literally needed to be a castle

Muchalls Castle, five miles north of Stonehaven, as engraved by R.W. Billings for the *Baronial and Ecclesiastical Antiquities of Scotland* (1845–52). As the panel set over the gate helpfully records, it was begun by Arthur Burnett of Leys in 1619 and completed by his son Sir Thomas Burnett in 1627. A splendid example of an L-plan, with a tentative return on one jamb, it still retains its barmekin wall. The triple gunloops on either side of the gate were almost certainly intended as a decorative feature.

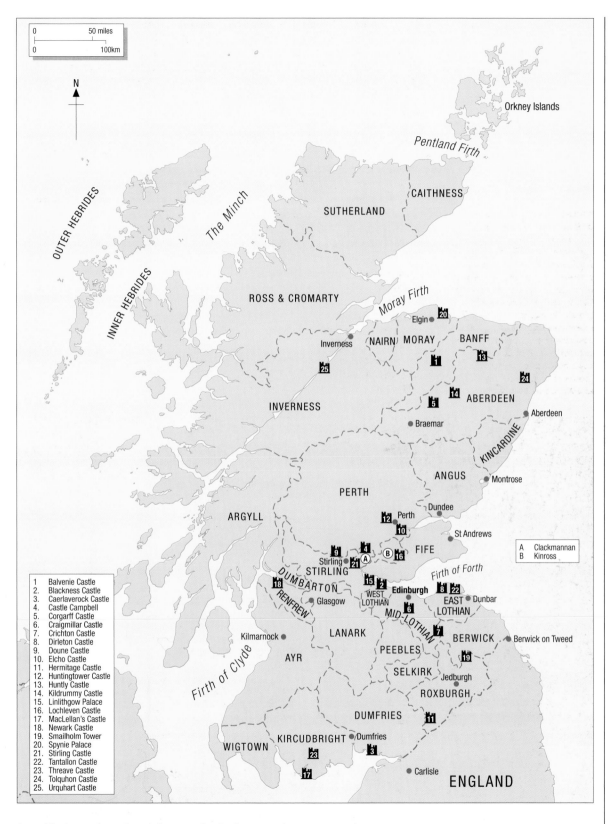

Scale:
0 — 50 miles
0 — 100km

N

Orkney Islands

Pentland Firth

CAITHNESS

SUTHERLAND

OUTER HEBRIDES

INNER HEBRIDES

The Minch

ROSS & CROMARTY

Moray Firth

Elgin • [20]

Inverness •

NAIRN MORAY BANFF

[25] [1] [13]

[24]

[5] [14] ABERDEEN

Aberdeen •

• Braemar

KINCARDINE

INVERNESS

ANGUS

Montrose •

PERTH

Dundee •

[12] Perth •

[10] St Andrews •

ARGYLL [9] [4] FIFE

Stirling • [21] (A) (B) [16]

STIRLING Firth of Forth

[15] [2] Edinburgh • [8] [22]

DUMBARTON [18] WEST LOTHIAN Dunbar •

RENFREW Glasgow • [6] EAST LOTHIAN

MID-LOTHIAN [7]

Kilmarnock • LANARK BERWICK Berwick on Tweed •

PEEBLES [19]

AYR SELKIRK Jedburgh •

Firth of Clyde ROXBURGH

DUMFRIES [11]

KIRCUDBRIGHT • Dumfries

[23] [3]

WIGTOWN • Carlisle

[17] ENGLAND

A Clackmannan
B Kinross

1   Balvenie Castle
2. Blackness Castle
3. Caerlaverock Castle
4. Castle Campbell
5. Corgarff Castle
6. Craigmillar Castle
7. Crichton Castle
8. Dirleton Castle
9. Doune Castle
10. Elcho Castle
11. Hermitage Castle
12. Huntingtower Castle
13. Huntly Castle
14. Kildrummy Castle
15. Linlithgow Palace
16. Lochleven Castle
17. MacLellan's Castle
18. Newark Castle
19. Smailholm Tower
20. Spynie Palace
21. Stirling Castle
22. Tantallon Castle
23. Threave Castle
24. Tolquhon Castle
25. Urquhart Castle

ABOVE The key castles and tower houses in Scotland mentioned
in the text. The county boundaries shown are the pre-1974 ones.

Chronology

1296–1314	First Scottish War of Independence.
1297	Revolt against English occupation begins with attacks on English-held castles, including Urquhart. English army defeated at battle of Stirling Bridge.
1298	Scots army defeated at Falkirk, but English still fail to hold Scotland.
1306–1308	Civil war in Scotland, ending in decisive victory for south-western-based Bruce faction.
1314	Robert I (The Bruce) wins battle of Bannockburn to end first War of Independence.
1320	Declaration of Arbroath asserts sovereignty of people.
1329	Death of Robert I.
1333	Scots defeated at Halidon Hill outside Berwick and Second War of Independence and civil war follows.
1335	Battle of Culblean, Aberdeenshire ending civil war.
1349–50	The Black Death.
1411	Battle of Harlaw outside Aberdeen marks beginning of final polarisation of Highland and Lowland Scotland.
1455	Fall of the Black Douglases.
1493	Forfeiture of Lordship of the Isles.
1513	Scots badly defeated at battle of Flodden, Northumberland.
1542	Scots defeated at Solway Moss.
1546	Scots victory in battle of Ancrum Moor.
1547	Scots heavily defeated in battle of Pinkie, outside Musselburgh.
1560	Siege of Leith by Anglo-Scots Protestant army.
1562	Catholics defeated at battle of Corrichie in Aberdeenshire.
1568	Catholics again defeated at battle of Langside, outside Glasgow.
1603	James VI of Scotland becomes James I of England.
1639–1660	Great Civil War, beginning in Scotland and effectively ending with surrender of Dunnottar Castle in 1652.
1689–1692	First Jacobite Rising.
1715–1716	Second Jacobite Rising.
1719	Third Jacobite Rising.
1745–1746	Fourth and last Jacobite Rising.
1746	Unsuccessful Jacobite siege of Blair Castle – the last one to be besieged in Britain.

ABOVE Crichton Castle, Midlothian, engraved by R.W. Billings for the *Baronial and Ecclesiastical Antiquities of Scotland*.

RIGHT Craigievar Castle, Aberdeenshire engraved by R.W. Billings. Built over a 25-year period between 1600 and 1627, by William Forbes, it was intended from the outset to be a gentleman's residence rather than a fortress.

Design and development

Broadly speaking Scottish castles fall into four basic categories. First there are the old Celtic fortresses, of which Edinburgh and Stirling are the most famous. These owed their importance to their strategic position and tactical siting, and were simply fortified by building an irregular trace around the perimeter of the site, within which a variety of buildings could be erected without regard to military necessity. Arguably some of the small Hebridean castles such as Mingary also fall into this category but with the exception of Urquhart, which for reasons of its own will be described in a later chapter, they mostly lie outwith the scope of this book, which is chiefly concerned with post-medieval fortalices. The other three types of Scottish castles are dealt with below.

Motte and bailey castles

In the second, and rather brief and transient category, are a surprising number of feudal motte and bailey castles which mostly survive only as earthworks. After its initial introduction early in the 12th century this type of castle spread rapidly throughout Scotland, though the greatest concentrations are to be found in Galloway, where the feudal system was first introduced in order to bridle the unruly clans of the south-west; and in Aberdeenshire, where a younger brother of William 'The Lion' (1165–1214) was granted the Lordship of the Garioch. This was castle building at its most cheap and cheerful: a simple earthwork mound or motte thrown up in haste (except where it was possible to utilise a naturally occurring glacial deposit) and topped with some kind of timber fortification overlooking a palisaded domestic enclosure called a bailey. Just as in England a few of these very basic structures did develop over time into more formidable structures, although a surprising number seem to have been abandoned within a very short space of time. Occasionally some of them, such as Duffus Castle in Morayshire, retained the original motte as part of a later stone structure (with unfortunate results at Duffus when the entire north-west corner detached itself as the earthwork collapsed under the weight), but during the so-called 'Golden Age' of Alexander II and Alexander III a number of strong enceinte castles were constructed in their place, featuring large round towers and high curtain walls, built of dressed ashlar or course rubble.

Enceinte castles and courtyard castles

The finest examples of these enceinte castles (the third type in our classification system) are to be found at Urquhart by Loch Ness; Kildrummy in Strathdon; Dirleton in the Lothians; Bothwell in Lanarkshire; and at Caerlaverock – which despite its odd Welsh-sounding name is to be found in south-west Scotland – although at least fourteen others of varying size and importance have been identified.

To a certain extent, therefore, castle building in Scotland at first followed the same pattern as in England, but the Wars of Independence at the beginning of the 14th century saw a sudden and complete reversal of the process. Early experience on both sides proved that, notwithstanding their undoubted usefulness, castles could rarely endure siege for any great length of time. This had two immediate consequences. In the first place, obviously enough, the English-held castles were captured one by one; and in the second place the Scots then declined to lock up fighting men in garrisons. Instead the castles were abandoned and slighted as a matter of course, and in some cases completely destroyed.

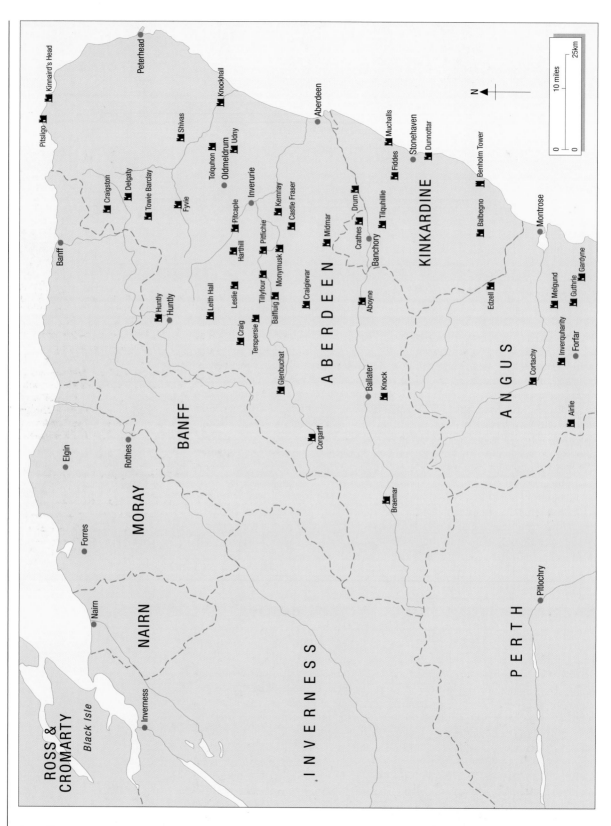

ABOVE This map shows the concentration of tower houses and castles in Aberdeenshire and the surrounding area.

10

Aberdeen provides a typical and indeed quite symbolic example. Since at least as far back as 1264 its status as a royal burgh had been marked by a modest but well-sited castle on a natural motte, dominating both town and harbour. One dark night in 1308, in the wake of Bruce's nearby victory at Barra, the Aberdonians demonstrated that they knew the winning side when they saw it by suddenly storming the place. Apart from the story that the citizens' watchword was *Bon Accord*, which ever since has been the burgh motto, accounts of its fall are curiously vague and although the castle is traditionally assumed to have housed an English garrison, its defenders are rather more likely to have been local men in the service of the recently defeated Comyns. If so there may very well have been rather more theatre than drama in the seizure, but there is no doubting that afterwards the castle was completely razed and replaced with a modest little chapel dedicated to St Ninian.

TOP LEFT An atmospheric photo of the rather unprepossessing gatehouse tower at Dunnottar Castle. Access from the beach is by way of a natural cleft in the rock, thoroughly blocked by the wall in the foreground and entered through what is effectively a door barely large enough to admit a small pack-horse.

TOP RIGHT Another atmospheric photo of Dunnottar Castle. This is an old Celtic fortress on a rocky headland, still featuring an extensive range of domestic buildings, largely dating from the 16th century. The tower house can be seen at the right.

Doune Castle as reconstructed by McGibbon and Ross. The outer wall is admitted to be conjectural and almost certainly represents an aspiration rather than actual construction.

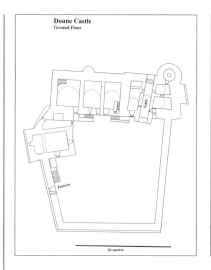

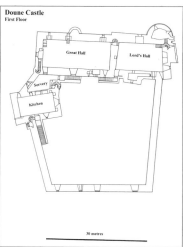

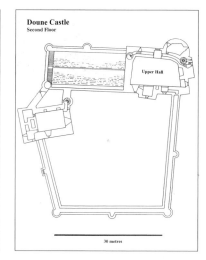

Top LEFT Doune Castle: a ground-floor plan. For the sake of clarity a range of minor domestic buildings erected along the east wall have been omitted since they did not form part of the original design and their purpose is uncertain. The circular chamber to the east of the gate was once thought to be an internal wellhouse, but excavations have found no trace of one. The actual castle well is in the centre of the courtyard.

Top MIDDLE Doune Castle: first-floor plan. An interesting feature of the design is the fact that the only direct connection between the tower house over the gate and the extension to its left is a small passage apparently inserted as an afterthought to link the so-called Lord's Hall with the Great Hall. The late W.G. Simpson opined this was because the inhabitants of the former distrusted the mercenary garrison housed next door, but in fact it appears to be a mundane reflection of the fact that the castle was built in modular stages with the great hall being bolted on to the tower house as it were, some time after it had been completed. Note the window openings in the south wall for a range of structures that were never built.

Top RIGHT Doune Castle: second-floor plan. As this plan emphasises, despite its outwardly large and formidable appearance, Doune did not actually boast a great deal of accommodation. Other than the two halls, there are effectively just two residential apartments, one on the top level of the tower house, and what must have been a rather cosy suite immediately above the kitchens.

This deliberate avoidance of large-scale fortification was a process which went on all over Scotland during the later middle ages. Most of the larger enceinte castles survived the Wars of Independence, simply because they were too substantial to be destroyed easily, but comparatively few were built afterwards, largely because of the virtual disappearance of the aristocratic magnates. Consequently, the later courtyard castles that developed from them, such as Doune and the great palace at Linlithgow, were usually either royal or quasi-royal establishments. Some of the great nobles did occasionally try to emulate them, but like the Crichtons and Douglases quickly found that over-mighty subjects had an unfortunate tendency to be quite literally cut down to size. Significantly, despite their outward starkness, nearly all of these 14th- and 15th-century castles were primarily dwelling houses rather than military fortresses.

Tower houses

Conventional castles were also the exception rather than the rule, since from the 14th century onwards it was the tower house (our fourth type) which became the dominant castle form, as expressed in 1424 when the Crown issued a 'licence and special favour to build a tower of fortalice of Dundas in the manner of a castle with the kernels (crenellations) etc. usual in a fortalice of this sort according to the Kingdom of Scotland'. Yet, once again for the most part Scottish tower houses were not really castles in the generally accepted meaning of the term, far less a development of the Norman donjon or keep, but rather were fortified houses, built on a comparatively modest scale by the people who would actually live in them. It would also be true to say that they were, using a Scottish term, defencible rather than defensive. In other words, while tower houses were obviously designed and intended to be defended if need be, they were not primarily designed or sited as military fortifications in a conventional sense. If some of them are strongly situated, most of them appear to have been sited more for convenience than necessity.

Tower houses soon proved to be a robust and highly successful design, used by kings and commoners alike. They were not by any means a poor man's substitute form of castle, and all that really separates the mighty towers at Borthwick and Dunnottar for example from the much cosier ones at Evelick and Kinkell is their relative size. Arguably even the large courtyard castles, of which Doune is probably the finest surviving example[1], were in effect oversized tower houses, rather than a development of the enceinte style.

---

[1] Stewart Cruden has argued in *The Scottish Castle* that Doune is actually a late enceinte castle; but the height of the towers relative to the perimeter and the way in which the south wall was built with large window openings clearly shows it was conceived at the outset as a courtyard castle, but finished as a tower house.

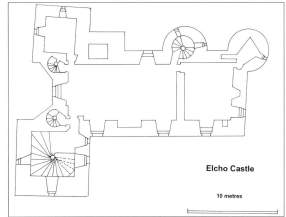

Over time three quite distinct basic styles of tower house evolved. It should be stressed however that ultimately all of them remained concurrent. Square or rectangular towers were the rule in the late 13th and 14th centuries, and for much of the 15th century, and only about a quarter of 15th-century ones were either built as L-plan, or at least converted to it very soon afterwards. However, although L-plan and the later Z-plan castles became increasingly common in the 16th and 17th centuries, the square or rectangular style never really disappeared.

Rectangular tower houses

The very earliest and most basic form was the peel tower, which was in effect a miniature donjon or keep, offering very minimal comfort but serving as a refuge in time of trouble. It was not necessarily capable of withstanding a proper siege but certainly up to keeping the owner and family safe from fast-moving raiders who could not afford to hang around much beyond daylight. This simple square or rectangular tower, which has parallels both with the ancient brochs and with the monastic refuge towers in Ireland (two examples of which can be found in Scotland at Abernethy and Brechin), survived longest in the Borders and for very good reason it is chiefly associated with that region. Peebleshire alone, for instance, reputedly boasted some 80 peel towers, of which only five now remain more or less intact and another 20-odd in more or less ruinous condition. Nevertheless, at one time peel towers could be found across much of Scotland. The Gordons' famous 'Peel of Strathbogie' at Huntly, Preston's Tower at Tolquhon, and perhaps also the old tower at Drum on Deeside, are good examples.

The very earliest peel towers and the tower houses that developed from them, dating from the second half of the 13th century, were simple square or more frequently rectangular structures, with anything up to four or five floors above a vault at ground level. Only a single example – Orchardton in Galloway, completed by 1456 – was constructed on a circular plan. The entrance was almost invariably at the first-floor level (though there are exceptions, such as Udny Castle), and one of the hoarier myths still told about them is that it was always accessed by means of a ladder for better security. It is possible this may have been so with some of the smaller border peel towers, but for most access was actually obtained by means of a wooden fore-stair, which could be dismantled or even burned in case of an emergency. Only then, rather than for everyday purposes, might a ladder be used as a temporary expedient instead.

TOP LEFT Elcho Castle near Perth, by R.W. Billings for *Baronial and Ecclesiastical Antiquities of Scotland* (1845–52), rather defies classification, having no fewer than five discrete projecting towers.

TOP RIGHT Elcho Castle, first-floor plan showing hall and adjacent solar. At first sight it appears to be a Z2 with haphazard additions, but it was clearly built this way from the ground up, sometime about 1570–80 – although the misalignment of the square tower at the north-west corner suggests an interruption.

BELOW Corgarff Castle, Strathdon: a simple rectangular tower house of four storeys and a garret, probably dating from the second half of the 16th century. Note the cap-house at the head of the stairs, providing access to the garret. The gables were probably crow-stepped originally, but smoothed when the castle was converted into a military post after the Jacobite Rising of 1745.

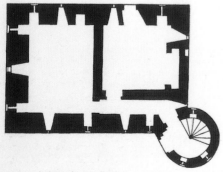

Kinkell Castle

Also known as Kinkell Clarsach, this very typical tower house in the Black Isle was begun in 1594 by John Roy Mackenzie and finished by his son Alexander in 1614. Ruinous for many years it was fully restored in the 1970s. In form it is probably best described as an L2, although the large flanking tower only contains a turnpike stair and all the living accommodation is within the three-storey main block. The inset illustration shows a plan view of the ground floor.

The fact of the matter is that while peels served well enough in troubled times, they were far too cramped and uncomfortable if conditions did not actually compel their use, and so away from the Borders there was a shift from fortresses to fortified houses, or tower houses.

Initially this may have been done simply by altering or adding to the upper storeys. Udny Castle in Aberdeenshire provides a fairly clear example of this, with the three lower floors nestling within very thick walls – some 8ft (2.5m) thick – and both the first and second floors resting on stone vaulting. Although Ranald of Udny had a charter for the lands from David II (1329–71), this part of the castle appears to date from the first half of the 15th century. The much more spacious and comfortable fourth and fifth floors are probably of the 16th century with early 17th-century embellishments.

Externally, most of these towers give a first impression of massive strength, but as with Udny the profusion of windows at various levels above the ground floor usually reveals a labyrinth of stairs, passages, closets and chambers built within the walls. Useful though these mural spaces might be, they were obviously limited in size by the original building footprint and the real solution to creating more spacious accommodation was simply to start all over again and build a completely new and much larger structure next to the original – as was done for example at Strathbogie, when the Gordons built a spacious hall tower next to their ancient peel, and advertised the distinction by re-naming it Huntly after their earldom.

L-plan tower houses

Such ambitious rebuilding was all very well for those who could afford it, but did not really address the problems faced by a laird who had a perfectly good tower which was in splendid condition but simply too small for his needs. Happily, sometime in the late 15th century, Scottish master-masons hit upon the idea of adding a jamb or wing, usually at right angles to existing structures in order to create extra living space on a more modest, or at least a more affordable, scale. Thus was created the L-plan, which became so characteristic of Scottish castle building.

Initially of course, being additions to existing towers and often done on the cheap with thinner walls, these jambs sometimes differed markedly in proportion and height from the original, and are obviously extensions. However, over the course of time L-plan castles came to be designed and built

Braemar Castle is perhaps the quintessential L-plan tower house. Although the present loopholed outer wall, like the near identical one at Corgarff, was actually constructed by the British Army after 1746, the tower house will almost certainly have been surrounded by an earlier barmekin wall of similar dimensions.

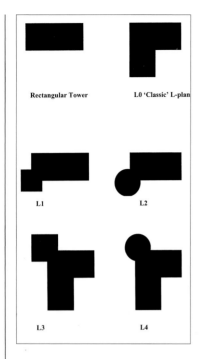

Rectangular Tower   L0 'Classic' L-plan

L1   L2

L3   L4

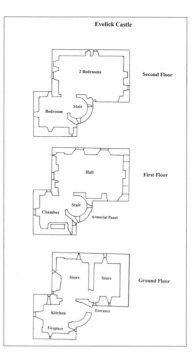

Evelick Castle

2 Bedrooms   Second Floor

Bedroom Stair

Hall   First Floor

Chamber Stair

Armorial Panel

Store Store   Ground Floor

Kitchen Entrance

Fireplace

TOP LEFT L-plan tower house typology; this diagram illustrates the four basic variant layouts on the 'classic' styles. In practice the actual proportions could vary quite considerably.

TOP RIGHT Evelick Castle, Perthshire. Built in about 1600 and now ruinous, this is a very typical example of the L1 tower house. The most striking feature is its modest size. The hall, at 10m by 5m, might be suitable for entertaining friends but hardly capable of hosting a banquet. It is, in short, a comfortable family house, not a fortress.

in that form from the ground up, and four different sub-styles can be identified as set out in the diagram on the left.

It should be stressed that this typology is of course entirely modern and would not have been recognised by 16th-century masons, and it relates only to the arrangement of the flanking jambs or towers. There was no consistency as to the relative proportions of each, or to the degree to which one was 'embedded' in the other, as will be plain from the individual ground plans scattered through this book.

The first of the major variants appeared in about 1540 when castle building began afresh as Scotland recovered from the effects of Flodden, where to all intents and purposes a whole generation of would-be castle-builders had been wiped out. Those L-plan castles built before Flodden invariably had the jamb projecting from one of the long sides of the main tower, in line with the gable end – a true 'L' shape in other words. After about 1540 or so it became much more common for the jamb to be offset, effectively becoming a flanking tower tacked on to one corner of the main tower rather than being integral to it.

Known as type L1, a fair number were conversions rather than new-build and it is difficult to see this particular development as anything other than a direct response to the widespread introduction of hand-held firearms. Up until this point the primary means of defending a tower had been by the simple expedient of dropping things onto attackers from a great height. Using guns effectively required a proper fire-plan and this in turn led to the offsetting of the jamb in order to provide the necessary flanking fire.

The earliest identified example of the L1 type appears to be Castle Levan in Renfrewshire, which certainly started off, unsurprisingly, as a rectangular tower. However when the Semple (or Sempill) family acquired it in 1540 they promptly added a large jamb, although their modernisation was somewhat undermined by giving the new wing the same inverted keyhole-type gunloops used on the original rather than the more up-to-date wide-mouthed style. Castle Levan may, however, have been something of an aberration, for a combination of heraldic and documentary evidence dates most L1 castles to the later period 1580–1630. Apart from Castle Levan, only Balfluig in Aberdeenshire, built in 1556, and Comrie in Perthshire, built the following year, seem to have anticipated the rush.

Type L2 was rather similar in concept, but very different in appearance. Once again the jamb was quite unambiguously a flanking tower rather than a wing, but this time it was a circular one. The L2 form also seems to date from the 1540s, for it was sometime around 1545 that the Earl of Huntly added a massive round 'drum' tower to one corner of his 'palace' or hall tower at Strathbogie. Once again this was supposedly done with firearms in mind and it has been suggested that the re-appearance of the early medieval drum tower was due to the influence of continental military engineers, hired by the Crown to construct artillery blockhouses at various coastal castles. It seems unlikely, however, that this was the case at Huntly, for although the Earl was of some importance as the King's Lieutenant in the north, neither the drum tower nor any other part of the castle is actually pierced for artillery. Be that as it may, between 1540 and 1560 round towers were added to the hall towers at Balvenie in Banffshire, Cairnbulg in Aberdeenshire, to the Bishop of Orkney's palace at Kirkwall, and to Newark in Fife, as well as at Strathbogie/Huntly; but once again the majority of the 20 known examples seem to have been built between 1580 and 1610.

Much less common were the rather curious and downright untidy L3 and L4 variants. At first sight most of these appear to have started off as classic L-plans, before having either a circular or a square tower added at the rear angle, though it is generally unclear as to whether this was indeed the case or whether they were designed and built this way from the outset. Only five examples of L3 castles are known: at the south-east corner tower of Balvenie (which is actually a much altered enceinte castle), at Dundarave in Argyllshire, Esslemont in Aberdeenshire, and at Killochan and Fernie (both in Fife). Similarly there are just four examples of L4 castles, of which the projecting angle towers at Bavelaw in Midlothian and Wester Greenock in Renfrew are certainly known to be later additions to conventional L-plans. Laurence Scott, for example, the laird of Bavelaw, was noted to have 'raised tua turrets upon the entrie thairof' in 1628. As to the other two, Cromarty Castle in Rossshire is said to date from as early as 1507, but if so that date can only refer to the original rectangular tower, rather than to the later extensions. Quite uniquely the projecting tower is set diagonally across the rear angle, rather than offset, which is the clearest possible indicator that it was a later addition. MacLellan's Castle in Kirkcudbright, on the other hand, dating from shortly before 1582, may be an entirely homogenous structure.

Z-plan tower houses

In time the L1 and L2 variants developed logically enough into the Z-plan castle, which effectively comprised a strong central tower with two smaller towers or jambs attached to diagonally opposed corners of the main structure, perhaps in order to provide interlocking fields of fire all the way around. For understandable reasons this style, in three variants, became very popular and of some 64 known examples, no fewer than 19 of them were built in the North-East of Scotland, between the Dee and the Spey, which strongly suggests that it may have originated there.

A word of caution needs to be inserted however in that while the term Z-plan is widely used to denote any house with opposed flanking towers, some

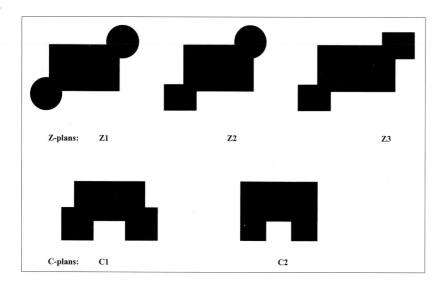

Z-plans: Z1   Z2   Z3

C-plans: C1   C2

Z-plan and C-plan variants. All five styles essentially feature a main rectangular tower with relatively small extensions on the corners.

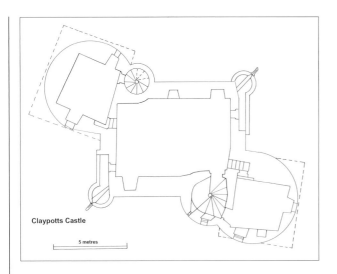

Claypotts Castle; third-floor plan. This is a 'true' Z-plan tower house with accommodation rather than turnpike stairs in the flanking towers. Note the random alignment of both the towers and the cap-houses at fourth-floor level.

of them may be nothing of the sort. Where a house such as Claypotts has two opposed jambs or wings containing living spaces, then it is quite unambiguously a Z-plan structure. However should one or both the flanking towers merely contain a stairway, then arguably it is still fundamentally a rectangular tower-house, or an L-plan. Huntly/Strathbogie is a good example of the latter, with its large drum tower on one corner and a small stair tower added on the opposing one in 1602. On that basis it could be classified as a Z-plan but in reality should still more properly be regarded as an L-plan.

The Z1 style features round towers on both corners, and perhaps one of the best-known examples is Claypotts, on the outskirts of Dundee. Dating at least in part from about 1569 (the date carved on one of the gables), and probably completed by 1588, it was originally built by the Strachan family, but later passed to the Grahams of Claverhouse. Another good example, which deserves to be better known, is Benholm's Lodging, built in Aberdeen in about 1600, probably as an L2 before having a second tower added at a later date. Similarly the Z2 variant was almost invariably a composite structure featuring a round tower on one corner and a square or rectangular one on the other. One of the finest examples is Castle Fraser in Aberdeenshire, which began life in the 15th century as a large rectangular hall tower, four storeys and an attic high. Subsequently, and presumably at different dates, a large drum tower was added – very similar in proportion and scale to the one at Strathbogie/Huntly dating from about 1545 – and then afterwards a square tower, of four storeys. A heraldic panel over the entrance bearing the date 1576 may relate to this particular stage of the building. Interestingly enough the Forbes' castle at Tolquhon in Aberdeenshire, although built around a courtyard, not only features a twin-towered gatehouse but has round and square towers on opposing towers in imitation of the Z2 style. Finally, the Z3 has square or rectangular towers on both corners but appears to have been the least common of the three. The earliest examples, such as Hatton Castle in Forfarshire and Tilquhillie on Deeside, seem to date from the 1570s.

C-plan tower houses

What appears at first sight to be another variant or pair of variants on the L-plan is the so-called C-plan, featuring two projecting wings or towers on adjacent rather than diagonally opposed corners. However, on closer examination there appears to be no military justification for them. The clue may lie in their earlier designation by architectural historians as E-plan castles, despite the absence of a central projection, for the inspiration may have been the contemporary English E-plan country house. One example of this style appears to be Borthwick near Edinburgh, constructed shortly after 1430, although there is considerable evidence to suggest that the two projecting jambs on the west side were originally matched by two others on the east side – until Cromwell knocked the place about a bit.

Although quite unambiguously tower houses, most C-plan castles, such as Craigston in Aberdeenshire built in 1607, were primarily built for comfort and display rather than as fortalices. So closely set were the projecting jambs of the C2 variant that in some instances, such as at Craigston, the gap between them was actually bridged over, while Borthwick comes with an apocryphal story that condemned prisoners were offered their freedom if they could safely jump across from one wing to the other.

T-plan tower houses

Finally there was the T-plan, which obviously enough comprised a rectangular tower house with a projecting jamb or tower set halfway along one face of the building, rather than at a corner. These projections might be square or rectangular (T1) or semi-circular (T2) and it was also possible to find the latter built into the back of what otherwise appears to be an L-plan tower house. Although classed as a discrete style it is arguable that it is nothing of the sort. In nearly all cases the projection is not really an accommodation block, but is very small and simply a means of providing a stairway external to the main structure, usually when an existing wooden fore-stair became inconvenient and it was thought desirable to provide an entrance at ground level instead.

Entrances, stair towers and cap-houses

The 're-entrant angle' or hinge of L-plan and Z-plan towers and the recesses of the C-plan also provided a secure position for a doorway (never a gate) at ground level, which from a domestic point of view was a considerable improvement over the old fore-stair.

Internal stairs connecting the various floors were almost always of the spiral or turnpike variety in order to save space, although there was a tendency in later castles to build wide, square, sectioned stair towers as the likelihood of having to defend them receded. Ordinarily turnpike stairs were ascended in a clockwise direction supposedly so that a defender retreating upwards had his unguarded left side to the wall while his attacker coming up from below had his sword-arm to the wall. Whether or not this did actually confer much of an advantage – or for that matter the opportunity to test it ever really arose – tradition holds that the Ker family in the Borders, who were notoriously left handed, built their stairs to rise 'widdershins' or counter-clockwise.

Originally stairs were contained within the thickness of the walling in rectangular towers, or at least tucked into a corner, but with the advent of the L-plan it became common to either build an external stair tower instead of a

BOTTOM LEFT Borthwick Castle at first-floor level, usefully illustrating the classic C-plan. Stewart Cruden in his classic book *The Scottish Castle* states that the two projecting wings on the west side were originally matched by two others on the east side, but that it was rebuilt as shown after the Civil War.

BOTTOM RIGHT The T-plan was really a variant on the basic rectangular tower house with a projecting wing set in the middle rather than attached to one corner. L/T is a similar variant on the L-plan.

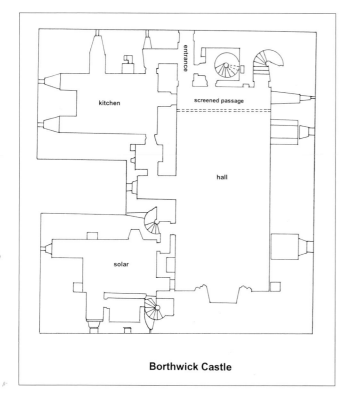

Borthwick Castle

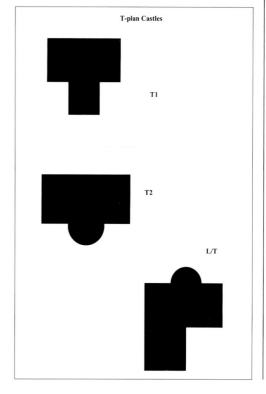

new wing, or to insert a stair tower, incorporating the ground-level door, into the re-entrant angle, as can be seen in the plans for Evelick in Perthshire on page 16 and in the photograph of Braemar on page 15. In addition it also became very common to attach additional external stair towers, corbelled out from the first floor or above, rather than from the ground floor as can be seen in the illustration on page 14, depicting Kinkell Castle.

In either case, since the stairs were peripheral to the living accommodation it was often necessary to provide a small cap-house at the stair head, in order to facilitate access to the garrets, which in turn could either be simple attics in the roof-space, or a discrete additional storey set within the wall-head parapet.

Cap-houses were square structures, irrespective of whether the stairs themselves were carried within a circular tower or within the thickness of the wall, and a good example of a cap house topping off a rectangular tower can be seen in the image of Corgarff Castle on page 13. They were not, however confined to stair towers and many of the circular wing towers attached to type L2, Z1 and Z2 tower houses had square cap-houses corbelled out on the top of them rather than conical roofs. Generally speaking, however, they are most commonly found topping off those flanking towers large enough to contain living spaces rather than the smaller ones enclosing a turnpike stair. Claypotts provides one of the best examples and it is a pity that, having been interrupted, the work was so obviously botched and the cap-houses badly misaligned.

Huntingtower Castle near Perth, engraved by R. W. Billings for the *Baronial and Ecclesiastical Antiquities of Scotland* (1845–52), was built by the Ruthven family in the 15th and early 16th centuries. Remarkably enough it was originally two quite distinct buildings: a rectangular tower on the right and a later L-plan tower on the left, separated by a gap of some 10ft (3m), until linked by a three-storey infill sometime during the 17th century.

Construction

Since the majority of Scottish castles were 'defencible' houses rather than fortresses, the siting of them was generally less critical than might otherwise have been the case. The old Celtic forts of Edinburgh, Stirling, Dumbarton, Dunnottar and Urquhart were as a rule situated on rocky outcrops and largely relied on the natural strength of their sites rather than on man-made defences. Some later castles in dangerous areas, such as the peel tower at Smailholm in the Borders, were also sited for security rather than comfort, but on the whole the majority of sites were more accessible than otherwise. An old motte might be utilised, as at Braemar, but the tower could equally well be planted in an open field, as at Udny or nearby Tolquhon. If it were situated close by a river, as at Huntly, that was simply with a view to enjoying good access to water and fishing rather than for protection. In short the primary consideration was comfort and convenience.

Indeed a number of tower houses were even built within the confines of towns. This was partly for security of course – the celebrated 'Cleanse the Causeway' affray in 1520, when the Hamiltons and the Douglases turned Edinburgh's High Street into a battlefield, being a salutary reminder of the need for something more substantial than a stout front door. Very largely, however, it was simply down to the fact that the tower house became such a well-established vernacular style that it was employed as a matter of course by the gentry when building their town houses. Therefore, while an English town might be dominated by a single feudal or royal castle, Scottish ones as far apart as Aberdeen and Jedburgh boasted a number of what were effectively private castles whose front doors opened directly on to the street.

Aberdeen is in fact very typical in this regard and both extant and recorded examples of urban tower houses include what is now known as Provost Skene's House in the Guestrow, which began as an L-plan tower house in 1545; Provost Ross's House in the Shiprow dating from 1593; Mar's Castle in the Gallowgate built two years later, and most remarkable of all, Keith of Benholm's 'Lodging' in the Netherkirkgate built in about 1600. Only the last perhaps, a Z-plan tower house, complete with gunloops set below many of the ground-floor windows, was unambiguously a fortalice, but otherwise there was very little indeed to distinguish these urban tower houses from those built in the countryside and in fact it is doubtful whether any real distinction between the two was actually recognised.

Structure

The construction of tower houses was straightforward with a very thick-walled basement or ground floor, subdivided into vaulted chambers, which served to support the living areas above. At this level the walls might be pierced for gunloops or very small windows, and there would usually be a pit prison in the

Coxton Tower; another engraving by R.W. Billings for the *Baronial and Ecclesiastical Antiquities of Scotland* (1845–52). This remarkable building dating to the early 17th century was built to be fireproof, all the internal flooring being of vaulted stonework. Accessing it by ladder as shown here was obviously highly inconvenient and originally there was no doubt a more substantial fore-stair.

An essential accessory to any castle or tower house was the doo-cot, or dove-cot – the Boath doo-cot on the old castle hill (the motte of a long-vanished feudal one) at Auldearn being a particularly fine example. Although young birds could be and were taken for food, this was very much a side benefit and the main purpose of doo-cots was actually to collect bird-lime for use in mortar for building and maintaining the fabric of stone structures.

thickness of the wall – hence the lairds' powers of 'pit and gallows' (i.e. to imprison or hang criminals). Up above, mural chambers are fairly common in older rectangular tower houses where space was very much at a premium, but rather less common once jambs and flanking towers were added.

Walls were invariably constructed of stone and there is not one single example of a brick-built structure despite the popularity of that medium for comparable English manor houses of the period. High-status towers, such as the royal castle at Borthwick, might be constructed of ashlar, which was not only expensive but time-consuming to dress and erect. It has been estimated for example that the tower house alone at Borthwick will have taken ten years to build, let alone fit out. Much more common therefore was the use of random rubble. While a skilled enough job in itself, the use of rubble did not require each individual block to be cut and finished by a stonemason. There was still inevitably some proper masonry work involved in cutting the mouldings for doorways, windows, fireplaces and of course the gunloops, but erecting a tower house was generally a job for a builder rather than a master-mason. It also meant that the actual mechanics of construction were much easier, requiring nothing more sophisticated than scaffolding and a bucket hoist for the rubble and mortar.

Generally speaking the rubble, which was simply gathered locally rather than quarried, came in large egg-shaped lumps that would be split in two by the practised application of a large hammer. The flat faces of the broken rock were then used to form the outward face of the wall, while the gaps in between are filled with smaller chippings. The whole lot was bound together with a lime mortar, either made from birdlime collected from dove-cots or crushed and burnt sea-shells. On higher-status buildings the same lime mortar could also be used to bind the rubble core of the wall, and if this was done an extremely solid structure would result, as can be seen at Duffus and Urquhart. At the former, as already mentioned, one corner accidentally broke away as a result of the old earthen motte collapsing beneath, while at Urquhart the top of the gatehouse was deliberately removed by the enthusiastic application of gunpowder. In both cases however the detached portions remained substantially intact and were merely re-located, albeit involuntarily.

On the other hand, if economy was a consideration then a clay-based mortar might be used for the core instead. This served well enough so long as the outer skin of the wall and the wall-head retained its integrity, but if allowed to deteriorate it would do so very quickly.

Although it was a good deal quicker and easier to use than ashlar, rubble was not without its drawbacks, the chief of which was its vulnerability to water penetration. This might in turn affect the structural stability of the wall itself, especially if it had a clay core, and was addressed in three ways. The first was to seal the wall-head with capstones to prevent rainwater seeping in from the top. The second was to thicken the base of the wall at ground level and top off this plinth about a metre above ground level with a string course – effectively a line of moulded beading with a 45-degree slope on the upper surface to deflect any water running down the wall away from the foundations. The chief defence, however, was harling. This is a very traditional finish used on the exterior of Scottish buildings, consisting of a thrown-on coating of lime mortar mixed with aggregate – quite different from modern pebble-dashing where dry aggregate is thrown onto a cement render. The harling, which could be an inch (25mm) or more thick, not only levelled off the otherwise rough face of the

LEFT Violence could often erupt inside a tower house, as seen in this contemporary illustration of the mysterious Gowrie affair in 1600, which saw an attempted kidnapping or assassination of King James VI – seen keeping out of harm's way on the right. Of related interest are the stout, inward-opening, wooden shutters to the windows in the background.

BELOW Udny Castle, Aberdeenshire as engraved by R.W. Billings for the *Baronial and Ecclesiastical Antiquities of Scotland* (1845–52). A simple rectangular tower house only a short distance from Tolquhon, it probably originates from the first half of the 15th century, was heightened in the 16th century (like Preston's Tower), and finally completed in the 17th century. Legend has it that it was built by three lairds of Udny, and ruined all three.

rubble wall, but also provided a semi-absorbent surface which not only protected it from rainwater but slowed the water running down the wall, so reducing potential erosion. Being semi-absorbent it also meant that it soaked up any water that penetrated cracks, and so allowed it to dry out rather than sealing it in.

Harling was often coloured to harmonise with the stonework exposed on details such as windows, gunloops, corbelling, parapets and so on. If the stone was red sandstone then sufficient dust and grit would be added to provide a pinkish colour; brown sandstone was complemented by the addition of cattle dung to provide an ochre colour; and granite was complemented by white harling.

Roofing

A variety of roofing materials might be used although the basic construction method was the same for all. In the sure and certain expectation of bad weather, roofs were always steeply pitched and enclosed by crow-stepped gables. This crow-stepping was not a decorative feature. Ordinarily of course the roof should overhang the gable in order to carry rainwater away from it, but while there was always a possibility of the roof leaking at this point if it was enclosed, it was a risk worth taking since otherwise there was every likelihood that strong winds might otherwise get under the edge and strip the roof off completely.

Round towers and turrets might sometimes have conical roofs, but generally speaking this only applied to smaller ones, especially if the top were partially inset into an angle. Otherwise, as described previously, there was a decided preference for topping them with square cap-houses with ordinary gabled roofs, topping them off with a flat roof as at Midmar and Castle Fraser. Very

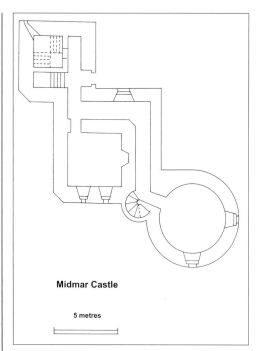

Midmar Castle

5 metres

The flanking towers of most L-plan and Z-plan castles are more or less inset quite snugly into the main tower, but at Midmar in Aberdeenshire, they seem almost semi-detached. Built at the end of the 16th century this Z2 is constructed with almost mathematical precision exactly on a north–south alignment. As at Castle Fraser the great drum tower is flat topped.

occasionally an inclined or lean-to roof was provided, as seen at Balfour Castle, an L2 near Kirriemuir in Forfarshire, though it is uncertain in this case whether this represents an ancient repair or whether the tower was never completed to its intended height.

As to the construction of the roof, the first task was always to put in the wall plate – a continuous strip of planking about 8in. (20cm) wide, sitting on the wall-head and into which the lower ends of the joists are pegged. The various beams, joists and rafters making up the roof structure seem to have been first assembled on the ground, for they are usually found to have roman numerals cut into them indicating their intended placing, and were then morticed and pegged together, apparently with tough pieces of tree root, rather than iron nails, which were susceptible to corrosion.

Conical roofs created their own problems and required a great deal of internal cross-bracing since they tended to open up and spread out at the bottom under the downward pressure of the slates. In order to hold the roof together it was necessary to butt the main joists on the inner edge of the wall-head, and then add a shorter secondary set butted off the wall-plate. The result was that the roof is thus given a pleasant, slightly convex, bell-shaped profile.

Once the joists and other wooden framing were in place, a solid skin of 'sarking' or wooden planking, tightly butted together, would be nailed on. With this foundation in place, the choice of outer skin varied considerably according to wealth and geography.

Slates

Slate is now almost universally seen on those Scottish castles still fortunate enough to possess a roof, but it is most unlikely to have been quite so common in the 15th and 16th centuries. Almost all Scottish slate came from the quarry at Ballachulish, which by virtue of sitting on the shores of Loch Linnhe was easily accessible by boat. It has an attractive blue colour, not unlike mussel shells, which also might account for its popularity. However, since the quarry did not open until about 1650, few if any castles can have used it as their original roof covering. The story is told that after the Scots army was routed at the battle of Inverkeithing in 1651, a party of Highlanders tried to take refuge in nearby Pitrievie Castle, but were driven off by slates showered down upon them from the roof. On first consideration this would point to an early date, if it were not for court proceedings relating to the alleged theft of materials from Urquhart Castle some 60 years later that referred to roofing 'slates', which were actually large pieces of lead sheeting about the size of a cow-hide. Clearly then the term slate had a much wider application and could be used to describe a variety of roofing slabs.

Urquhart Castle, obviously, was roofed in lead and no doubt a great many others were as well. It was certainly versatile and easy to use, but it was also expensive and in the longer term prone to leaking as its own weight could cause it to 'creep' downwards and so open up the fixing holes. The other alternatives were largely dictated by local circumstances. Where the building was sufficiently solidly constructed to bear the weight, particularly if it had vaulted upper storeys, large slabs of Caithness stone or even sandstone might be pegged onto the roof. Similarly, if suitable clay was available reasonably close by then flat pottery tiles could be produced and nailed directly on to the inner skin planking. Another alternative was wooden shingles, but by far the most common solution, surprisingly enough, was to use heather thatch. Although this presented obvious hazards in the admittedly unlikely event of an attack, it was cheap, practical and provided good insulation. In fact as late as the mid-18th century even the military barrack blocks at Fort Augustus were thatched in this fashion rather than tiled.

Windows

It goes without saying that windows were something of a balancing act, offsetting the undoubted advantages of light and air against the possibility of someone or something rather more unpleasant coming through. As a general rule, therefore, the size of a window was directly proportionate to its height above the ground. Glass, moreover, was expensive in the medieval period and consequently any glazing set into these windows will have been made up of small pieces held together with lead or with wooden astragals. Cheaper substitutes included parchment of horn, but in any event the windows were invariably fixed in place and could not be opened – largely to avoid draughts. Reformers trying to persuade 19th-century soldiers and sailors not to block up the ventilators provided for barrack rooms and mess-decks were invariably told that the occupants got fresh air enough when they were outside. Much the same attitude seems to have prevailed amongst the residents of many castles. If there was a requirement for opening a window, whether for ventilation, or simply to look out – or to spot for the musketeer using the gunloop often set below – a small wooden shutter would take up the lower half of the window opening. All too often, some of the smaller castles had no glazing at all and simply relied on full-length wooden shutters.

Floors

Vaults are essentially arches, which if built properly can be extremely strong. In most Scottish castles dressed stone was rarely used and instead the arch was constructed of flat slabs, usually of sandstone, which can be most readily split in that fashion. As these slabs were not wedge-shaped there was very little locking and only very slight outward movement in the walls could be enough to bring about a collapse. Nevertheless the first floor was invariably vaulted, sometimes the top floor and occasionally those in between as well.

Those floors carried on vaults, as well as any mural chambers, were therefore flagged or tiled, but otherwise floors were wooden and supported on beams approximately 8in. (20cm) square. These beams in turn rested upon corbels, which at first sight appear to be relatively short stubs of stonework projecting from the wall. In fact the visible part is merely the decorative end of a fairly long piece of dressed stone extending by as much as two feet (60cm) into the thickness of the wall. Manoeuvring a beam into such a deep slot will have been all but impossible, and so they must have been laid in as the stonemasons were actually building the wall.

Internal walls and details

Any internal stonework was covered up as much as possible, in order to reduce condensation. At first sight plaster might seem the obvious choice, but it came late to Scotland and consequently was rare in tower houses. The first recorded use was at the outset of the 16th century, when James IV's queen, Margaret, ordered various rooms at Holyrood House and Stirling to be so covered. Naturally enough this royal example was afterwards emulated elsewhere, but only by those who could afford it, such as the Earl of Huntly, and very notably 'Danzig Willie' Forbes of Craigievar, whose plasterwork ceilings are justly celebrated.

These, however, were very much the exception and another alternative was wainscotting or carved wooden panelling. A very common vernacular style still popular in Scotland simply consisted of cladding the wall with moulded (but otherwise plain) fir planking, and it is more than likely that this was employed in many tower houses both for covering stonework and for internal partitioning. This was certainly the case at Urquhart Castle where a court case

Strengthening of Blackness

Blackness Castle began simply as a tower house owned by the Crichton family, but in 1444 their main seat at Barnton, near Edinburgh, was burned during a feud with the Earl of Douglas. By 1449 they had moved to Blackness and enlarged it by the addition of a curtain wall and the accommodation block now forming the base of the south tower. Just four years later, however, the Crichton lands were forfeited and it was seized by the Crown. As the port served the nearby royal burgh of Linlithgow and Linlithgow Palace – the principal residence of the Stuart kings – the castle was then strengthened to a near unprecedented degree.

The inset at lower left shows the castle in plan view. The main illustration shows a cutaway view of the south tower; the original structure is shown in red; the strengthening work carried out by James Hamilton of Finart between 1537 and 1542 is in orange; and the subsequent work is in yellow. Note particularly the long 'gunholes' (1) inserted as part of the works. Essentially Finart turned the south tower into a near solid blockhouse. Then, probably in the 1560s, a 'spur' was added on the west side (2). This was not intended to add to the fortifications as such but was rather to create a new and more defencible entrance. Even if the outer gate (3) was carried, any attacker was then faced with a dog-leg passage raked by fire from a thoughtfully placed caponier (4), before reaching the entrance proper (5).

A very similar entrance, covered by a quite excessive number of gunloops, was built at Dunnottar Castle around the same time. The upper part of the spur (6) was added in the late 17th century.

Tolquhon Castle. The largely ornamental 16th-century gatehouse at once demonstrates the easy balance between fortification and comfort. The lower part of the twin towers flanking the gate are pierced with double gunloops, but the upper part features large windows calculated to admit plenty of light, while – very typically – defended with heavy iron grilles to deter intruders.

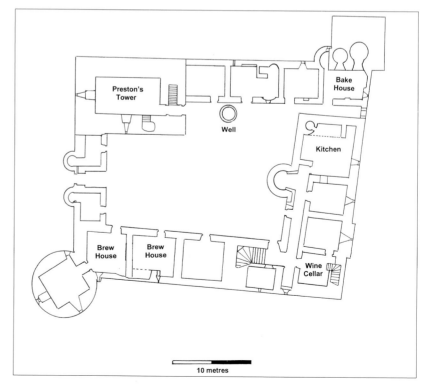

Tolquhon Castle: ground-floor plan. The extremely solid-looking Preston's Tower is the oldest surviving part of the castle, a simple four-floored tower house probably built by Sir Henry Preston, the then Lord of Formartine, at the beginning of the 15th century. After his death the castle passed to the Forbes family, and the quadrangular range was added by Sir William Forbes of Tolquhon in 1584. This no doubt replaced a pre-existing range of ancillary buildings on much the same site, and although outwardly very warlike in appearance is very much a country house rather than a fortress. The slightly whimsical nature of its design is also apparent from the way two towers have been built on opposing corners in imitation of the Z2 plan.

Preston's Tower

Bake House

Well

Kitchen

Brew House

Brew House

Wine Cellar

10 metres

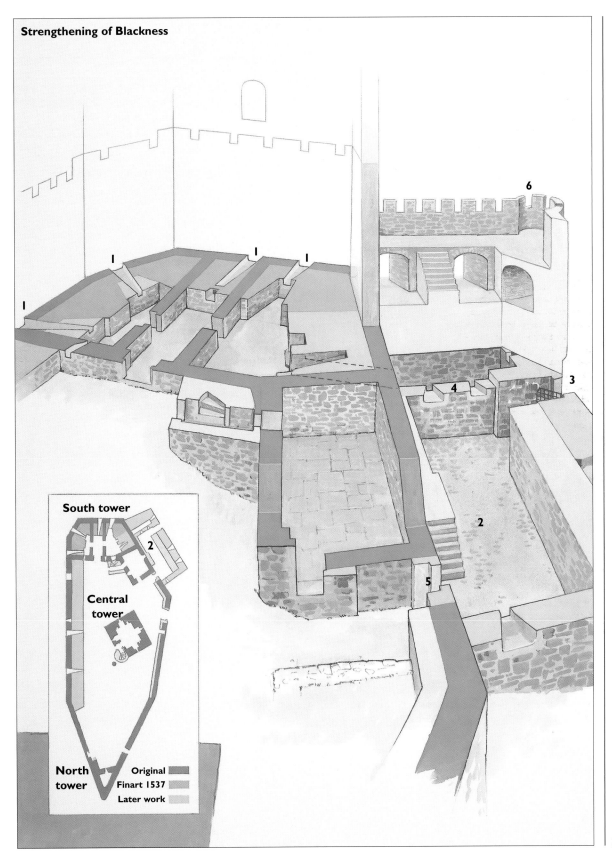

South tower

2

Central tower

North tower

Original
Finart 1537
Later work

6

3

4

2

5

described later involved the theft of 'deals' or planks and wooden partitioning. The advantages of this wooden cladding and partitioning were that it was not only easier and quicker to apply, maintain, and replace than plasterwork, but it was once again far less susceptible to condensation and damp, especially when the room was heated up to any considerable degree in cold weather.

The extent of internal partitioning is not always apparent, particularly where floors have disappeared. Empty halls stripped back to the stonework can give a false impression of large and draughty spaces, but may in fact have been filled up by a cluster of smaller and cosier wooden-partitioned chambers. The likelihood of some kind of subdivision can certainly be inferred by the presence of deep recesses in walls, too large to be aumbreys or built-in cupboards, as well as by more obvious clues such as wall sockets.

Where halls were indeed used as such it was also usual to have a wooden screen across the bottom end, partly to guard against draughts and partly to provide a service area as an interface between the kitchen and the hall. If this were on the same floor as the kitchen, there would usually be serving hatches connecting the two. Other kitchen accessories included the obligatory oven, and most also had sluices to dispose of kitchen waste directly through the wall rather than physically carrying it outside.

Sometimes, as at Kinkell, the sluice worked the other way so that fresh water could be poured rather than carried inside. Wells are rarely to be found integral to tower houses, largely through a simple lack of space, although interestingly enough Benholm's Lodging in Aberdeen was long known as the 'Well-house Tower'. Instead wells were normally found outside in the courtyard, unless a conveniently situated stream, river or loch provided an excuse not to go digging deep holes. At first sight this might appear to be something of a weakness in military terms, but of course the smaller towers were never intended to stand a proper siege.

A similarly casual attitude was adopted towards human waste disposal. Once again the larger castles boasted the usual mural privies or 'bog houses' of one kind or another for the quality, normally in the form of the ubiquitous garderobe chutes. Sometimes these were corbelled out and discharged relatively high up the wall, with unsightly results, but otherwise they were built in the thickness of the wall and sealed with a 'grund-wa' stane' – a stone plug – until the time came to clean it out. In 1571 Corgarff had been burned when a treacherous servant, known only as Jock, removed the plug and stuffed the chute with combustibles. Whether for the sake of security against similar attempts, or more simply to avoid the uncomfortable effects of an updraft on a windy night, some garderobes were nothing more than a discrete chamber equipped with a bucket, as can still be found at Dunnottar.

All too often, however, even such rudimentary facilities were lacking and instead the family would rely on chamber pots, which would be unceremoniously emptied straight out of the window, perhaps accompanied by the traditional cry of 'Gardey Loo!' (supposedly derived from the French 'Gardez l'eau!') heard in the Edinburgh 'lands' – or perhaps not. The intended destination of the contents was usually the large midden or muck heap maintained within the barmekin wall, and nearly all of the servants resorted directly to this as a matter of course. As late as the 18th century, more than one English visitor would comment on how it was common to see people of both sexes and all ages come out of their houses in a quite shocking state of undress to begin their day squatting on the dung-hill.

Tolquhon Castle: the main domestic range. As is often the case the prominent tower is not a defensive feature, but simply houses a stairway.

Principles of defence

It would be fair to say that the Scots took to gunpowder and its instruments – pistols, hagbutts (arquebuses) and muskets – with an unwonted enthusiasm, which was reflected in both the design and detail of most tower houses. Initially, as we have seen, towers were simple rectangular affairs defended simply by dropping missiles from a great height onto anyone congregating below. The introduction of firearms, however, although not in themselves responsible for the advent of the classic L-plan, certainly brought about its variants all the way through to the Z-plan as builders strove to eliminate blind spots and achieve interlocking fields of fire. At the same time, firearms quite obviously influenced the detail in the matter of gunloops, sometimes appearing singly and sometimes in an intimidating multitude to cover vulnerable points such as entrances. Nevertheless they were still intended for little more than close defence; the basic defensive principle remained one of sitting tight and hoping the attackers would go away.

Occasionally, if the owner was wealthy enough to afford such luxuries and the castle large enough to justify them, light cannon might be used. The splendidly wicked Patrick Stewart, Earl of Orkney, certainly had something of a passion for guns and one contemporary described how:

> his pomp was so great there that he went never from his Castle to the Kirk, nor abroad otherwise, without the convoy of fifty musketeers and other gentlemen of convoy and guard; and similarly before dinner and supper there were three trumpeters that sounded still until the meat of the first service was set at table and similarly at the second service and consequently after the grace. He had also his ships directed to the sea to intercept pirates and collect tribute of foreign fishers that came yearly to these seas; whereby he made such collection of great guns and other weapons for war as no house, palace or castle, yea in all Scotland, was furnished with the like.

Whether many artillery pieces of any description ended up in other private dwelling houses as distinct from royal castles is a moot point, but an inventory of the contents of Tolquhon Castle compiled by Sir William Forbes in December 1589 does mention his 'artalyerie': four long slim bronze guns bearing his arms, monogram and motto, *Salus per Christum*. They are, however, very much decorative pieces and in keeping with his almost whimsical castle, which, like Bodiam in Sussex, is 'an old soldier's dream house, irrelevant to [16th-century] warfare.' Earl Patrick aside, private artillery was very rare indeed and the plain fact of the matter is that with the exception of a handful of royal castles, usually on coastal sites, it was not envisaged that tower houses would have to contain or cope with artillery.

Artillery

The reason is not hard to find and is perfectly summed up by some routine paperwork from the English Civil War. On 16 May 1643 a warrant was issued by the Royalist ordnance office at Oxford for the assembling of a small train of artillery to be sent into the West Country. This was to comprise one brass cannon (a 12-pounder) and a brass mortar piece, with 50 and 24 rounds of ammunition respectively. This, as it happens, would have been the very minimum requirement for any gunner intent on knocking lumps off a Scottish

Defensive features

It was common for entrances to be surmounted by a heraldic panel displaying the arms of the owner, and the royal arms as well if he held his lands directly from the king. The heraldic entablature at Huntly Castle (**A**) is, however, quite exceptional and originally featured Huntly's arms, the royal arms, the five wounds of Christ, and the Risen Christ in Glory, finally topped off by an armoured St Michael. The doorway was secured by an interlaced iron yett (**B**). Also shown are a typical selection of gunloops (1–7). Note how most of them have small windows just above, presumably for sighting or spotting. (**1**) Ravenscraig, Fife, 1460; (**2**) Affleck, Forfarshire, late 15th century; (**3**) Tillycairn, Aberdeenshire, late 16th century; (**4**) Tolquhon, Aberdeenshire; (**5**) Muness, Shetland, 1598; (**6**) Muness, Shetland, 1598; (**7**) Leslie, Aberdeenshire, c.1661.

ABOVE Provost Skene's House, Aberdeen: the entrance. The original tower house is on the right and would have been entered from a door at the foot of the stair tower. Both of the projecting jambs date from 1626 or later.

TOP RIGHT Provost Skene's House, Aberdeen. The original part of the building, dating from 1545, was a fairly modest L-plan tower house, seen at the left of the photograph. Subsequent building work in 1626 and 1669 not only extended it to the right and raised it by another floor, but also added another, taller L-plan tower on the end. The arched gateway is a much later addition transplanted from a quite different property.

RIGHT Provost Skene's House, Aberdeen: a rear view. Once again the evolution is quite clear, with the original block in the centre, the 1626 addition on the right, and the 1669 enlargement on the left.

Defensive features

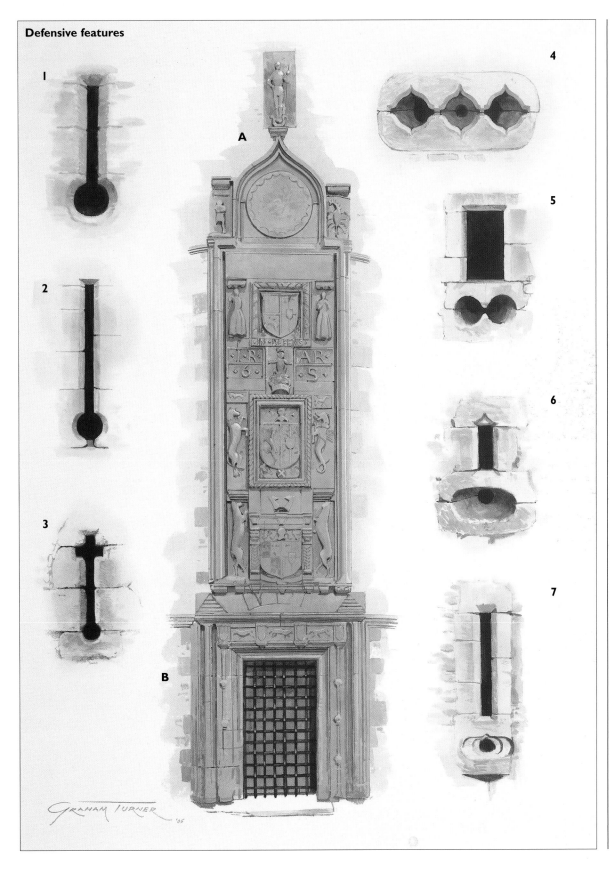

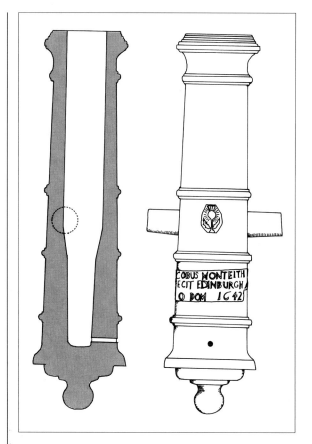

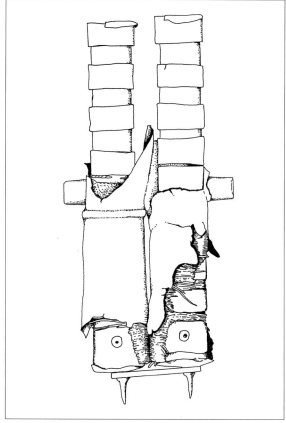

Top left The difficulty of transporting artillery overland across most of Scotland meant that cannon generally had to be capable of being pack-mounted. Guns such as this diminutive 3-pounder cast by James Monteith in Edinburgh in 1642 posed little threat to most castles.

Top right Light cannon such as this double-barrelled 'leather gun', one of a number made by James Wemyss in 1650, were obviously of no use for attacking tower houses, but could prove very useful as cheap anti-personnel weapons when defending them. A number of castles feature double or splayed gunloops close by their gateways, which could have accommodated pieces like this.

tower house, but moving it required all of two four-wheeled wagons, ten carts, 67 draught horses and nearly 100 men including a carpenter, a wheelwright and a blacksmith.

Furthermore, moving this heavy train of vehicles across the roads of Southern England was one thing; moving them over Scottish roads was all but impossible. The fact of the matter was that the quality of the roads linking Edinburgh with the North of England was very poor, but there were none north of the Forth, or at least none worthy of the name. Anything carried overland for any distance was carried on pack-horses and if too heavy for that it had to be carried by sea. A knock-on consequence was that even if cannon became available by whatever means, it was all but impossible to find those 67 or so draught horses strong enough to pull the guns and their associated equipment. The heavy Clydesdale breed still lay in the future and all that were available were riding horses and ponies. Even when the Scottish kings moved their guns they had to rely upon slow-moving oxen.

In short, both in terms of the capital costs involved and the sheer difficulty of moving guns anywhere across Scotland, bringing a train of artillery against a castle was something which only the king, or at least central government, was capable of. Facing cannon was thus generally a prospect that could be viewed with some equanimity by master-masons. Royal castles in coastal locations such as Blackness (see the illustration on page 27) or Ravenscraig in Fife might be massively strengthened to resist cannon fire – indeed an English intelligence report from 1543 bluntly described Blackness as 'impregnable' – but this was out of the question for private dwelling houses inland. All that could be done in an emergency was to hastily throw up or strengthen an external wall to shield it from direct artillery fire, in much the same way that additional skirting was fitted to German tanks during World War II.

Spynie Palace, near Elgin as engraved by R.W. Billings for the *Baronial and Ecclesiastical Antiquities of Scotland* (1845–52). A very large tower house, built by the Bishop of Moray between 1461 and 1482, and prudently incorporating a useful assortment of gunloops including the old-fashioned key-hole type in the foreground and the very large one in the main block to the left.

The most remarkable example of this occurred at Threave Castle in the 15th century when its Douglas owners fell foul of the king. At first sight the castle seems something of an oddity, an apparently isolated rectangular tower built around 1369 by Archibald the Grim and surrounded by what has been described as an 'artillery wall; with keyhole and dumb-bell gunloops and circular bastions at the angles'. Excavations have revealed, however, that originally the tower was surrounded not by a wall but by an extensive collection of domestic buildings, all of which were demolished as the royal army approached in 1455, and their stones hastily re-used to build the wall. In the event it was only partially successful, for the artillery train brought against it included the famous Mons Meg and extensive damage was done to the artillery wall. Nevertheless, it served its purpose insofar as little damage was done to the tower house itself, and eventually the garrison was instead bribed into surrender.

A similar story occurred at Haddo Castle in the 17th century, where the existing barmekin wall was strengthened, as will be described in a later chapter. Strictly speaking the barmekin wall was not a defensive feature at all, since it was invariably thin, rarely very high and almost never boasted a parapet. All that this was actually intended to do was provide a secure enclosure for what was in effect no more than a farmyard, in which cattle and other livestock might be securely penned in 'interesting times'. How much notice was taken of the statute (see page 6), both so far as building a barmekin wall in the first place, or conforming to this specification, is open to question. At any rate, once cattle rustling ceased to be a problem the barmekin wall was one of the first features to disappear, which is why so few now survive. They simply became inconvenient. Oddly enough, however, they did enjoy a brief revival when certain tower houses were taken over by the British Army in the wake of the Jacobite Rising of 1745; what are in effect barmekin walls angled and loopholed for musketry can still be found surrounding Corgarff and Braemar Castles.

Gunloops

The earliest style of gunloops were simply adaptations of the well-established vertical arrow slit, enlarged at the bottom by the addition of a slightly larger circular hole, calculated to allow a gun barrel to be poked through it. The limited traverse of this transitional gunloop, referred to as the 'inverted keyhole' style, is all too apparent and it soon gave way to purpose-designed gunloops.

ABOVE As a rule Scottish castles were not designed to withstand artillery fire; this earthwork ravelin constructed at Huntly Castle during the Civil War period is thus extremely rare.

RIGHT Noltland Castle, Westray engraved by R.W. Billings for the *Baronial and Ecclesiastical Antiquities of Scotland* (1845–52). A Z3 tower house, rather longer than most, built by Patrick Stewart, Earl of Orkney at the end of the 16th century and boasting a quite extraordinary number of gunloops – probably not unconnected to the fact that he never stirred abroad without an escort of 50 musketeers.

Naturally enough the precise form varied both according to the size of the weapon intended to be fired from it and the individual ideas of the builders, but at its most basic level a gunloop could be a single block of dressed stone bored through the centre with the requisite hole, which was then splayed both inside and out in a horizontal ellipse in order to allow as much traverse as possible. This was important, for as a rule gunloops were set very low in the wall in order to search out any attackers trying to crowd into blind spots at the bottom. There was no need for gunloops at higher levels since muskets and pistols would simply be discharged straight out through the ordinary windows.

This same basic design was employed for both hand-held firearms and for small cannon, although the latter tended to be provided with a horizontal slot rather than a round hole in order to aid traversing, or perhaps to permit the use of double-barrelled cannon. These were something of a Scottish speciality and feature quite prominently in Paton's sketches of the battle of Pinkie in 1547. Double-barrelled guns also enjoyed a brief and inglorious revival in the late 1640s when the then Master Gunner of Scotland, James Wemyss, introduced a range of so-called 'leather guns' (actually wrought-iron tubes tightly bound with cord and then skinned with leather) intended as close-range anti-personnel weapons.

Over the course of time the external moulding on these gunloops could become more elaborate but the only real design development was an increasing tendency to set them in pairs, threes or even in fours, particularly when covering the approaches to doorways and entrances. The tactical thinking – other than the sheer intimidatory effect of so many gaping firing ports – is not entirely certain, for they are set too closely together for two or more weapons to be discharged simultaneously. More likely it was simply to allow them to be fired in turn, and in quick succession, as one was thrust forward while the other was withdrawn to be reloaded. How four or more loops were to be used is more problematic, yet they do exist as for example at Dunnottar.

Most of the other defensive features of tower houses were also rather more in the nature of crime prevention measures than dictated by military science. Doors were of course solid affairs and almost always doubled with a solid inner one of reinforced oak, and an outer yett or wrought-iron grating. Similarly, external windows were primarily intended to let light into rooms rather than provide a useful means of showering missiles onto an attacker. They therefore tended to be large and consequently required to be protected by wrought-iron grilles.

Tour of a castle: Urquhart

Standing on an irregular promontory on the shores of Loch Ness, Urquhart Castle is unusually large in Scottish terms. However, the archaeology of the site as well as the more tangible architectural remains and documentation show it to have been in continuous use since early Pictish times right up until its final abandonment at the very end of the 17th century. As a result it manages to incorporate most major features of Scottish castle design and construction on its sprawling site.

The main defensive perimeter is not unlike a figure 8 in plan, or more accurately perhaps a very irregular letter B, with two quite distinct enclosures or baileys, joined more or less in the middle by the main entrance. Very conveniently the history of the castle and its architecture can thus be 'read' in three distinct phases, moving northwards from the earliest castle in what is now known as the Upper Bailey, through the later enceinte castle of the so-called Nether Bailey to the 16th-century tower house on the very northern end of the promontory. Once again, however, it should be stressed that these designations are modern ones which may not have been recognised by those who actually lived and worked there.

The Upper Bailey

Chronologically, an examination of this particular castle therefore needs to temporarily ignore the main entrance and begin instead with the Upper Bailey, situated on a high rocky knoll forming a natural motte on the southern part of the promontory. The remaining wall fragments here are low and difficult to interpret, but the presence of vitrified material in the ground indicates that this was the site of the original Pictish fort or dun. Typically these forts were ringworks situated on hilltop sites, with rubble walls that were initially stabilised by wooden cradling. At some point this cradling was burned and the resultant heat was sufficient to melt or vitrify the rubble into solid masses. Opinion is still divided as to whether this was a genuine, albeit eccentric, building technique or merely a by-product of the fort's later destruction by enemy action. On the one hand the effectiveness of deliberate vitrification is very hit and miss, being just as likely to damage as to strengthen the wall, but on the other hand the presence of vitrified material on these sites is pretty universal. All things considered, however, the balance of probability must lie with it being a by-product of deliberate destruction after capture, and as it happens Urquhart was to be captured with quite monotonous regularity throughout its long history.

Other than the presence of this material and various artefacts in the archaeology, there are no remaining traces of the Pictish dun. Aside from the footings of the contour-hugging curtain wall, there are essentially three medieval structures on this part of the site, at three different levels. On the landward side, and occupying the highest point of the castle, is a small compound with a rather untidy trace, measuring approximately 50m by 25m and incorporating a building or tower of some description at either end. This compound almost certainly represents the remains of the first medieval castle, built some time after 1230 by a royally connected Norman knight named Alan Durward. As he also happened to be the Earl of Atholl, a claimant to the Earldom of Mar, owner of Bolsover Castle in Derbyshire, and by all accounts the real power behind Alexander III, Urquhart probably came fairly low down his list of priorities. Nevertheless, given the rocky nature of the site, this castle must have been constructed of stone from the outset, which probably explains its survival during the Wars of Independence.

At the lowest level, almost completely filling a fairly narrow shelf overlooking the loch is a fairly long rectangular building, once two storeys high, which excavations have revealed was used at least in part as a smithy. This is almost certainly associated with the later castle forming the Nether Bailey, but although linked with it by way of the obligatory water-gate opening on to the loch, it is very much tucked away behind it, as is the circular doo-cot (or dove-cote) on the middle level, which will have provided the lime needed for building and maintenance works.

The Nether Bailey

After Durward's death in 1275, ownership of the castle passed to the Comyn lords of Badenoch and Lochaber, and they appear to have been responsible for the construction of the enceinte castle forming what is now known as the Nether Bailey, lying below Durward's castle on its natural motte. Although it is possible that this part of the site may have been occupied before, the Comyns built what effectively amounted to a completely new enceinte castle, with a 'service area' incorporating the original one discretely tucked away to one side and separated from it by a short stretch of curtain wall linking the main block with the gatehouse.

Exactly when this castle was built is uncertain, thanks to the extensive robbing out of its walls and the loss of dateable features. The Wars of Independence effectively began not with William Wallace's celebrated, if overblown, raid on Lanark, but with an unsuccessful attempt by Badenoch's nephew, Sir Andrew Moray, to retake Urquhart from an English garrison in June 1297. Afterwards Edward I gave orders that the castle was to 'be so strengthened and garrisoned that no damage may in any way occur to it' – which rather suggests that although regarded as important, the castle was not particularly strong and this might in turn point to its still being Durward's little fortress up on the rock. At any rate, by the time Edward gave those orders the castle was already back in Scottish hands and although the shifting fortunes of a complicated war saw it (unsuccessfully) held against Edward by one of the Comyns' men (Sir Alexander de Forbes in 1303), they all made their peace with him in the following year and it almost immediately reverted back to Sir Alexander Comyn of Badenoch. Sir Alexander in turn lost it to Bruce's men five years later – this time for good.

Notwithstanding its chequered history, it seems on balance likely that the new castle was already in existence during this period, for while a considerable amount of money is known to have been spent on Urquhart after the wars, it all relates to repair and maintenance rather than new building – so clearly it had been constructed sometime before the Comyns' final defeat by Bruce in 1308. The question is, just how long before?

Making due allowance for the irregularities and uneven nature of the site, the general arrangement of the Nether Bailey does in fact very closely correspond with that of Kildrummy, another Comyn stronghold, begun during the reign of Alexander II sometime before 1249. However, the dominant feature of this 'new' castle is the twin-towered gatehouse, similar to others built around the turn of the 13th and 14th centuries by a Savoyard architect, Master James of St George, who also designed the great Edwardian castles of North Wales, such as Conway, Harlech, and Caernarvon. In Scotland he was certainly responsible for the gatehouses at Linlithgow in 1304, and (significantly) at Kildrummy, so it is not improbable that he worked at Urquhart as well; and it is just possible therefore that the building of the so-called Nether Bailey was a direct response to troubled times. On balance, however, it is rather more likely that it was already in existence by 1297 and that, as at Kildrummy, the gatehouse alone was reconstructed by St George as part of the strengthening ordered by Edward.

Viewed as a discrete structure, the new castle is roughly oval in plan, though this reflects the geography of the site rather than any deliberate design. It has

Urquhart Castle

The present ruined state of Urquhart Castle makes a detailed reconstruction difficult, but this illustration shows its probable appearance in the early 17th century, by which time all building work on the site had ceased. There were in effect three different castles on the site, as distinguished by the coloured areas on the plan view – although there was of course some overlap as use continued to be made of the older elements throughout the castle's occupied history.

(1) Alan Durward's original castle; the roof-lines are conjectural, but the castle comprises a small tower house, hall, and bailey. (2) Doo-cot in Upper Bailey. (3) Smithy and workshops. (4) Early 14th-century gate-tower and barbican. (5) Combined prison and latrine block. (6) Site of drawbridge. (7) Great Hall and associated buildings belonging to late 13th-century/early 14th-century enceinte castle. (8) Unidentified building on hillock in middle of Nether Bailey; possibly a chapel, although more likely a detached tower predating the enceinte castle built around it. (9) Possible estate office associated with Grant of Freuchie's tower house. (10) 16th-century tower house, as finally completed in 1627.

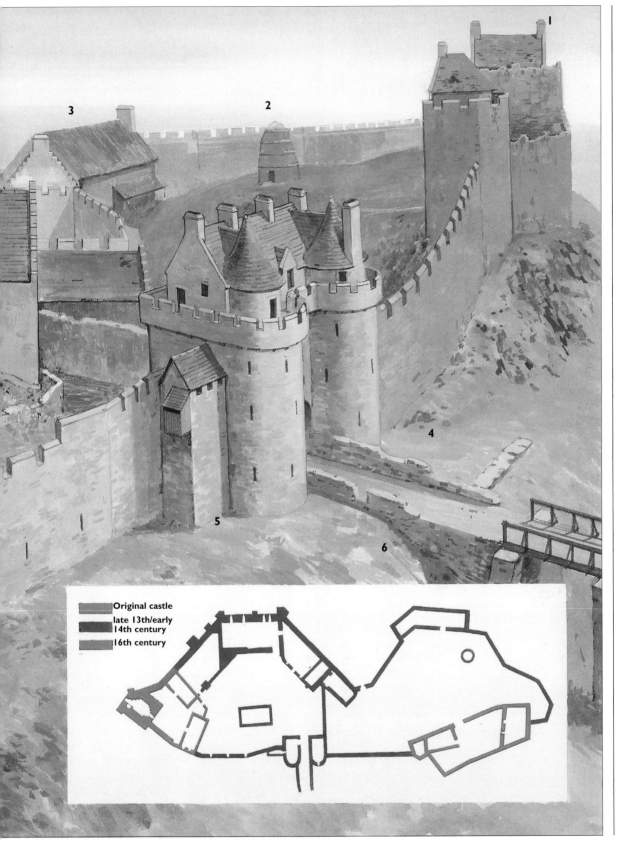

Original castle

late 13th/early
14th century

16th century

a large keep gatehouse at the front and the remains of what was probably an impressive range of buildings at the back, sitting immediately above the loch and commanding splendid views across it.

Immediately in front of the castle, on the landward side, is a great ditch cut into the natural rock, some 30m wide and 5m deep, spanned by a stone causeway, with a drawbridge about halfway across. Once over the drawbridge any visitors, friendly or otherwise, were then funnelled into a barbican, which was essentially a high-walled but roofless corridor leading directly to the gatehouse. The latter at first sight appears to be eccentrically offset to one side rather than planted in the middle of the curtain wall as one might expect – and as is the case at Kildrummy. In fact this location was forced on the builders by the existence of another rocky knoll inside the bailey.

The gatehouse

More than just a fortified entrance, the gatehouse was once a very formidable structure in its own right and appears to have originally been some four storeys high (although absolute certainty is difficult since the top of it was blown off in 1692 – and deposited more or less intact immediately in front of the gate). It provided the lodgings for the keeper or constable, as well as the usual offices at ground level. The entrance proper, running through the centre of the tower, is effectively a tunnel, secured at the outer end by a portcullis or drop-down gate and then two sets of timber doors, one opening outwards and the other inwards. This double-door system not only provided an additional obstacle to any attacker coming knocking at the front entrance but also ensured that the all-important gatehouse could still be defended if the perimeter was breached elsewhere. Interestingly that part of the passage between the portcullis and the doors was left unvaulted and roofed over with timber decking. It has been suggested that this was to allow the insertion of a number of trapdoors which could be used to drop missiles or noxious substances on any attackers jammed below, but in reality it was probably done in order to ease the installation and maintenance of the portcullis and its winding gear. If the portcullis had to be replaced it was obviously going to be easier to rip up a timber floor to create the necessary working space, in order to get the old one out and the new one in, than if it was all built of solid stonework.

On either side of the entrance passage are two self-contained lodges, the one on the south side contained a corn-drying kiln (perhaps the one which John Grant of Freuchie was required to provide in 1509), while the north side was evidently the guard-room with a narrow prison cell attached. Rather cruelly, this penal offshoot lay immediately underneath the lavatory and latrines for the constable's lodgings! Those lodgings were comparatively spacious, even if allowance is made for the portcullis mechanism at first-floor level. The surviving fragments show that there were two main rooms in each tower, each with its own fireplace, linked by two rather smaller rooms over the entrance passage, one of them housing the winding gear. Presumably the same arrangement was carried on in the floors above as well.

Ordinarily, having passed through the gate tunnel, visitors to most castles, whether friendly or otherwise, would find themselves in a reasonably level courtyard. Unlike its sister castle Kildrummy, Urquhart's main courtyard or bailey has a high and steep-sided rocky knoll right in the middle of it – which might argue against this area having formed part of Durward's original castle. Still extant on this knoll are the foundations of a rectangular building which has been interpreted as a chapel, although the fact that it is laid out on a north–south axis would suggest otherwise and it is hard to find another example of a chapel as a completely detached building. Its central position recalls the siting of the stable block within the courtyard at Strathbogie/Huntly, though the fact that it sits on top of a steep knoll would probably rule out that particular function. It is in fact possible that it was a tower serving as an outwork for Durward's castle, but there is simply no direct evidence of the building's function, its date, or for that matter whether it was ever completed.

Between the base of this knoll and the loch, arranged as half of a hexagon, in order to best fit the site, is the main range of buildings. Effectively, all that now survives are the ground or basement levels, once taken up with the kitchen and large storage areas, but the chambers above will have included the great hall and the usual domestic apartments associated with it, and it would be here that the chapel would normally be found, with its east window looking out over the loch. The present window remains are too fragmentary to do more than indicate their position (with those overlooking the loch pleasantly large), but if Kildrummy can once again be taken as a model, they were most likely plain lancets with wide splays, corner shafts, roll-moulded capitals, moulded heads in square orders, and scansion arches springing from miniature corbels.

After the Comyns' defeat in 1308 the castle passed for a time to Thomas Randolph, Bruce's Earl of Moray, but on the death of Randolph's grandson in 1346 Urquhart had reverted to the Crown and thereafter steadily declined in importance. It had already outlived its usefulness, for there was no need for a castle of this size in this particular location. It was simply too large and too expensive to maintain and man adequately on the off-chance that the MacDonalds would revive their dreams of hegemony over the mainland as well as the Isles. Inevitably, this meant that it was captured with ease when they did just that in 1395, and Charles MacLaine of Lochbuie was installed as its keeper. Although Donald of the Isles was badly defeated at Harlaw in 1411, Urquhart continued to be ravaged by marauding gangs professing allegiance to the Lords of the Isles, the Earls of Mar and even the King until in 1476 the MacDonalds were forced to relinquish the Earldom of Ross. The Earl of Huntly was then charged with restoring law and order, but by this time both castle and glen had been totally devastated and three years later Huntly leased them to Sir Duncan Grant of Freuchie.

The tower house

The Grants did their best, and in 1509 Sir Duncan's grandson, John Grant of Freuchie, otherwise the Laird of Grant, was given the lordship of Urquhart directly from the Crown. At the same time he was required to:

> repair or build at the castle a tower, with an outwork or rampart of stone and lime, for protecting the lands of the people from the inroads of thieves and malefactors; to construct within the castle a hall, chamber and kitchen, with all the requisite offices, such as a pantry, bake house, brewery, ox house, kiln, cot, dove grove, and orchard, with the necessary wooden fences.

However, at first Freuchie had little opportunity to carry out his instructions, for the death of the king at Flodden in 1513 prompted Sir Donald MacDonald of Lochalsh to make yet another attempt to re-establish the power of the Lords of the Isles. Naturally enough, in the process he ravaged Glen Urquhart and captured the castle, although Freuchie had it back again by the end of 1516. By way of compensation he was awarded £2,000 – but never saw a penny of it. In 1527 the chronicler Hector Boece commented that 'In this country [the old Earldom of Ross] was the famous castel of Urquhart of quhilk the rewinous wallis remains yet in gret admiration of pepill.' Clearly Freuchie had not yet been able to do anything much in the way of renovations to what, even at that date, was obviously still an impressive structure.

Then in 1545 came what may have been the last straw, when the MacDonalds once again captured the place, carrying off beds, bolsters, blankets, sheets, pots, pans, brewing vats, roasting spits, doors, yetts, tables and other furniture, guns, powder and armour. Yet although the castle was thoroughly

The tower house at Urquhart Castle

The tower house built by Grant of Freuchie is a typical rectangular one with a vaulted cellar (**1**) below the ground-floor hall (**2**), a vaulted top floor (**3**), and two intermediate wooden floors in between creating another room (**4**). For comparison, a section through Elphinstone Castle is provided (**5**), showing a slightly different arrangement of floors and a greater use of mural chambers. Elphinstone is also unusual in having an entrance at ground-floor level. Urquhart is more typical in being accessed at first-floor level (**6**), although the sunken ground floor means that a fore-stair is unneccessary. At the very top of the tower is a garret room (**7**), a turret chamber (**8**), and the roof features a defensive platform (**9**). The base of the tower is protected by a ditch (**10**). An inset illustration (**11**) shows the construction methods used for the cap-house roofs.

Another typically sprawling Celtic fortress, Urquhart Castle has been considerably modified over the years in line with changing military fashion. This photograph not only shows its magnificent setting but also demonstrates the extent to which it is dominated by higher ground.

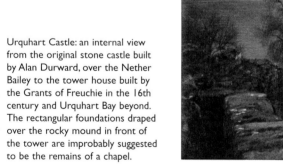

Urquhart Castle: an internal view from the original stone castle built by Alan Durward, over the Nether Bailey to the tower house built by the Grants of Freuchie in the 16th century and Urquhart Bay beyond. The rectangular foundations draped over the rocky mound in front of the tower are improbably suggested to be the remains of a chapel.

stripped out and a chest containing £300 Scots taken as well, it seems a pretty meagre haul. Be that as it may, this was to turn out to be the last time, but the ease with which a mob of clansmen were able to repeatedly walk into the castle is a clear demonstration of the fact that it was simply too big to be defended without a proper and ruinously expensive military garrison. Thus, all the indications are that the works eventually carried out by Freuchie and his sons were pretty largely confined to the upkeep of any usable accommodation and to the building of what was effectively a third castle on the site – the tower house.

The tower house at Urquhart Castle

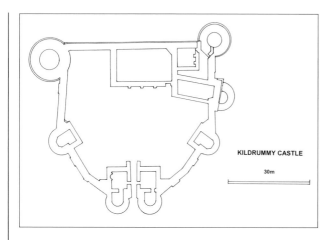

Kildrummy Castle, Strathdon. The layout of this Comyn stronghold in what is now regarded as a Highland area bears a remarkable resemblance to that of the so-called Nether Bailey at Urquhart, the only substantive differences being those imposed by the geography there.

KILDRUMMY CASTLE

30m

The tower house stands on the northern tip of the promontory, overlooking Urquhart Bay. The massive thickness of the basement walls indicate that there had already been a tower of some kind on the spot, at least since the later 14th century, possibly forming a part of the Comyns' enceinte castle. It would certainly correspond with the placing of the donjon tower at Kildrummy, although the latter is circular rather than square in plan. At any rate the present building unquestionably dates from the 16th century and interestingly enough is set within its own 'close', a small cobbled courtyard walled off from the rest of the Nether Bailey. Sharing the close are two quite ruinous rectangular buildings, the original functions of which, like so much else about the castle, are unknown. One of them, butting up against the old enceinte block, may have been a kitchen or other service area, and it is extremely tempting to speculate that the other may in fact have served as an estate office. Although the 1513 charters had also provided lands in Glen Urquhart for Freuchie's younger sons, thus establishing the cadet houses of Glenmoriston, Corrimony, and ultimately Shewglie, their early experiences seem to have put the Chiefs of Grant off the place. Most of their landholdings remained across on Speyside and so for much of the year the castle may only have been occupied by their factor.

One final pointer to the 'withdrawal' into this area is the presence of a rock-cut ditch within the close, protecting the entrance to the tower house. Quite clearly, although some use may have continued to be made of the older accommodation, perhaps for storage, the defensible part of the castle was henceforth limited to the tower house and its close (which may well be the 'outwork' envisaged in the 1509 charter), and ironically enough it is possible that some of the older parts of the castle may have been robbed of stone to build it. It may well be significant that in 1647 reference was made to the 'mansione and maner place of Wrquhart', which suggests that a distinction was then being made between the two elements.

The accommodation within the tower house itself is certainly modest enough, comprising a basement or 'vault' and just three chambers set one on top of the other, and subdivided with wooden partitioning. There is a servants' garret at the very top surrounded by a wall-walk and cap-houses, which are almost certainly the work of a master-mason named James Moray, who was working there in 1623.

Ruin

He was almost certainly the last to do so. The castle played no part in the otherwise tumultuous Civil Wars of the mid-17th century, although there is the usual melancholy note in 1647 that Urquhart had once again been plundered of all its 'plenishing, goodis and geir.' Nor did anyone attempt to hold it against Cromwell's men, while they displayed no interest in occupying it either, preferring instead to build a fort at Inverness and set a patrol boat on the loch. It did, however, enjoy a last brief moment of glory during the first of the Jacobite risings at the end of the century. The loyalties of the Laird of Grant's Glen Urquhart tenants and relations were ambiguous. Most of them, being realists, had begun looking to the nearby MacDonnells of Glengarry for leadership rather than their own absent chief, which ought to have placed them in the Jacobite camp. However, James Grant of Shewglie and his brother were murdered by a rebel foraging party, and so the glen became – or rather remained – something of a no-man's land, unprotected by the government and harried by the Jacobites. In an effort to restore law and order, three newly raised companies of regulars, numbering no more than 200 men, led by another Captain James Grant, were thrust into the castle and promptly besieged by Glengarry. For once in its existence, perhaps because it had an adequate garrison for a change, the castle held out. Although greatly outnumbering the defenders, Glengarry had no artillery and so had to content himself with a blockade, which proved ineffective in the end – the garrison being re-supplied by boat at one stage.

Unfortunately, when the military necessity for its presence disappeared in 1692, so did the garrison, and just to make sure that no-one else walked in, Captain Grant proceeded to blow up the gatehouse. So solidly built was it that instead of demolishing it completely all he actually succeeded in doing was to blast off the upper part and deposit it in a lump in front of the entrance. The Laird of Grant was unimpressed and said so, but although he had the promise of £44,000 in compensation, it was never paid and thereafter the castle was effectively abandoned, its decay being considerably hastened by some of the locals. One of them, Alexander MacUisdean Glass from nearby Buntait, was subsequently prosecuted for ripping out part of the internal fabric and the details of the case throw an interesting light on this. It was alleged that:

> there was taken from the vaults of the Castle of Urquhart ... ten ton cake lead and two thousand pound weight each ton, which ten ton lead was a pairt of the lead with which the said Castle of Urquhart ... was covered; as also, about the same time before mentioned [1708] there was taken furth of the said Castle, some deals or parts of the partitions of the chambers in the said Castle, which lead and deals being for some time amissing, and diligent search made for the same, there was found of the said ten tons of lead and quantity of timber or deals, in the said defenders their houses and barns in Buntait, or in their possession

As this was in 1717, nine years after the event, the search cannot have been too diligent, and by this time the 'defenders' had very enterprisingly used 'all the said deals or partitions, or at least a part of them, for making chests, girnels [oatmeal bins] or some other household or necessary materials.' As those materials were clearly lost beyond recovery Grant claimed compensation of:

> one shilling Scots per pound for every pound of the said ten tons lead, computing two thousand pounds weight to each ton, extending in all to one thousand pounds Scots money, as also six shillings Scots for each deal of the said two hundred deals being partitions, extending to sixty pounds Scots money foresaid.

Various witnesses were then compelled to testify, including Farquhar Urquhart who was 'objected against, that he cannot repeat the Lord's Prayer, Creed, and Ten Commandments, which he did'; he went on to testify that he made a chest for Glass, and was told by him that 'the timber was of the deals of the Castle of Urquhart ... (and) were formerly made up either lofting or a partition'. He claimed to know nothing of the lead, but Donald Noble usefully enough described having seen 'two pounds of lead, in the form of a slate, and in the form thereof, and about the thickness of a cow's hide' in Glass's byre.

Notwithstanding these and other 'evidences', the proceedings were eventually dropped, and in the meantime so too had the castle's tower house; for in February 1715 it was rather sadly reported that 'the Castell of Urquhart is blowen down with the last storm of wind, the south-west side thereof to the laich woult [low i.e. basement vault]'. One hopes the absence of the lead roofing did not contribute to this collapse, but whatever the cause or contributory factors it was at any rate the end of the castle.

Everyday life in the castles and tower houses

The late Professor Douglas Simpson commented that the typical medieval house consisted of a central hall, with kitchen and offices at its lower end and the owner's private rooms at the upper, and that the tower house is nothing more than a specialised form of hall house, simply up-ended for reasons of security. Life in a Scottish tower house was therefore remarkable only in its ordinariness, for its defensive features were not military in a conventional sense, but designed simply to protect those living inside from sudden attack by raiders and bandits rather than by armies.

This is charmingly illustrated by one of the garderobe or toilet chambers at Dunnottar Castle, situated immediately above a steep and inaccessible cliff overlooking the sea. There was never any possibility of an attack from that quarter and yet there is a pistol port set into the wall. This seeming paradox is however explained by the fact that it is set sufficiently low for the occupant of the chamber to sit at his ease, contemplating his lot, and pleasantly passing the time by shooting at the seagulls!

Such eccentricities aside, there are interesting parallels between the domestic arrangements of rural tower houses and urban tenements. Indeed, in describing life in a Scottish castle it should once again be stressed that the great majority of them were first and foremost family homes rather than fortresses and so had no requirement for a conventional military garrison. It is necessary to re-iterate this because the late but still influential Professor Simpson was much taken with the notion that many castles, most notably perhaps Doune, were specifically designed so as to completely segregate the quarters for the hired soldiers, or *lanzknechts* as he called them, from the family apartments, which could then if necessary be defended against any mutiny or treachery on the part of those mercenaries (assumed as a matter of course to be unreliable and prone to such disturbances), as well as more conventional external threats.

The ground level was invariably given over as storage space or working areas. There were good reasons for this. The combination of the solid masonry and vaulting needed to support the structure above; the small windows required for security; and the frequent absence of a damp course, all conspired to ensure that these chambers were at once uncomfortable places to live and yet ideal for the storage of many foodstuffs, particularly beer, vegetables and preserved meat. It was also, obviously, easier and a good deal more practical to access and store heavy and bulky items at this level than higher up, especially if the upper flooring was of timber construction.

It was largely in order to avoid this cellarage as much as for security reasons that the entrance to the house proper was often located at the level above, and accessed by means of a timber fore-stair irrespective of whether it was a tower house or a town house. Once inside it, the arrangement of the accommodation was closely linked to status in so far as the more elevated someone was socially, the higher up the building they were to be found. This was famously true of the towering Edinburgh 'lands', but even in a relatively modest tower house, domestic staff and day visitors were largely confined to the lower floors while the owner of the premises strove to be as high above them as possible, not least because the increased security meant that larger windows could be provided, making the upper apartments much lighter and airier than those below.

The people who lived in these tower houses varied considerably in social status, but not necessarily in character. An English traveller, John Taylor, described a typical laird in 1618:

The splendid heraldic entablature over the front door of Huntly Castle as engraved by R.W. Billings for the *Baronial and Ecclesiastical Antiquities of Scotland* (1845–52) dates from 1602 and is easily the most magnificent surviving example of its kind. Originally the carvings would have been brilliantly painted, but were somewhat defaced by a Captain James Wallace of Auchans who was offended by the imagery during the castle's occupation by Covenanting troops in 1640.

the master of the house his beaver [hat] being his blue bonnet, one that will wear no shirts but of the flexe that grows on his own ground, and of his wives, daughters or servants spinning; that hath his stockings, hose and jerkin of the wool of his own sheepes backes; that never (by his pride of apparel) caused mercer, draper, silkeman, embroiderer, or haberdasher to break and turn bankrupt; and yet this plaine homespunne fellow keepes and maintaines thirty, forty, fifty servants or perhaps more, every day releeving three or four score [60–80] poore people at his gate; and besides ali this can give noble entertainment for four or five dayes together, to five or six Earles and Lordes, besides Knights, Gentlemen and their followers, if they be three or four hundred men and horse of them; where they shall not only feed but feast, and not feast but banket.

If this seems exaggerated it is worth noting that in 1590 Campbell of Glenorchy's household got through 90 cattle, 20 pigs, 200 sheep, 424 salmon, 15,000 herring and 325 stones (2,275kg) of cheese, besides the usual staple of

Huntly Castle from the south, again engraved by R.W. Billings for the *Baronial and Ecclesiastical Antiquities of Scotland* (1845–52) and providing a good view of the upper works added in 1597. These were supposedly inspired by the Chateau de Blois, which Huntly had visited while in exile after the battle of Glenlivet. In a remarkable reversal of fortune he was not only allowed to come home in 1597, but raised to the dignity of marquis, since James VI needed him to maintain control of the north. Huntly thereupon proclaimed and celebrated the fact by carving (and probably painting) his name and title over the oriel windows: GEORGE GORDON FIRST MARQVIS OF HUNTLY, and below them the name of his wife; HENRIETTE STEWART MARQUISSE OF HUNTLY.

oatmeal and various other foodstuffs. The important point perhaps was that other than a very limited selection of luxury goods, such as a solitary sugar loaf, all of this, like the clothes he wore, was his own produce or that of his tenants paid over as rent in a cash-poor society. As another traveller noted in 1598:

> The Gentlemen reckon their revenues not by rents of monie, but by chauldrons of victuals … The Scots then living in factions used to keepe many followers, and so consumed their revenue of victuals, living in some want of money.

While Walter Forbes of Tolquhon had a large room in his castle given over as a library this was quite exceptional, for most lairds had little time for such idle luxuries. The majority of their time was spent out of doors and when the seven sons of Alexander Gordon of Knock were slain by Forbes of Strathgirnock and his men, they were not innocently engaged in any of the gentlemanly pursuits which might have been enjoyed by their English counterparts: they were attacked and murdered while digging peat.

A typical day in the life of a Scottish nobleman appears in an account of the Earl of Huntly's death in May 1576, where after waving off his sister and her husband, the Earl of Sutherland, he went off hunting, killed three hares and a fox and then came home to dinner. So far so good, but he then had a furious row when he decided to have a kick-about and no-one could find a football. In the end one of his servants was sent out to buy one, while he himself sat down to dine with his brother Lord Adam Gordon, and the Laird of Grant (alias Grant of Freuchie). What they ate is not recorded, but one visitor recalled eating at a Knight's house:

> who had many servants to attend him that brought in his meate with their heads covered with blew caps, the Table being more than half furnished with great platters of porridge each having a little piece of sodden [boiled] meate; And when the Table was served the servants did sit down with us, but the upper messe insteede of porridge had a pullet with some prunes in the broth.

Doubtless Huntly's last meal was something similar and over dinner he discussed 'ane appointment' involving the Laird of Cowbardie, and then all of them – and no doubt sufficient of their followers and servants to make up the numbers – went outside for the deferred game of football. It was all very informal, and all the more unfortunate therefore that in the middle of the game Huntly suffered a fatal heart attack.

After the owner's immediate family came a fairly transient group of kinsmen who might be genuinely related by blood, or more distantly by name, or simply men who were bound to the laird by a band of man-rent. The size and permanence of this group varied a great deal. In larger households, such as that of the Earls of Huntly, some of them might actually lodge in the castle for indeterminate periods of time, whilst at the other end of the scale the kinship, whether actual or presumed, might simply provide justification for dropping in for dinner unannounced. Sometimes the band of man-rent specifically referred to an obligation to be part of the laird's household, though it is almost always either for a specified period or from time to time, and often involved the man's own servants as well. This was the case for a certain David Liddall, who bound himself to Thomas Maule of Panmure: 'I havand honest sustentation and household of the said schir Thomas quhen I lykis to tak it for myself a servand man and tua hors.'

The status of servants and retainers could be ambiguous. On the one hand there was Thom Dawson of Paisley who undertook in 1536 to bring a servant with him to work as a gardener at Kilravock Castle near Inverness. Cooks and housemaids were similarly quite unambiguously servants and probably slept in the kitchens and garrets respectively, but less clear was the status of retainers, who were 'kept' but not employed. In 1546, for example, John Brisbane of Bishopton made a band with the Master of Boyd to 'ryd or gang with him in his household'. These retines not only provided the laird with a circle of trusted advisers and confidantes, but more importantly served to advertise his status, protect him from casual violence by his enemies and, conversely, could intimidate anyone who crossed him from the king on downwards. In fact successive acts tried, without evident success, to limit the size of such retines. In 1590 it was ordered that no earl coming into Edinburgh should bring more than 12 men, no lord more than eight, and no baron more than five. What was more they were all to be unarmed. This undoubtedly inspired more mirth than adherence and just seven months later the limits were doubled and nothing said as to whether or not they should be armed. Although outwardly there might appear to be parallels with the English system of livery and maintenance, there was, interestingly enough, no question of them being liveried: they served the laird – and played football with him – as friends and kinsmen, not as indentured servants.

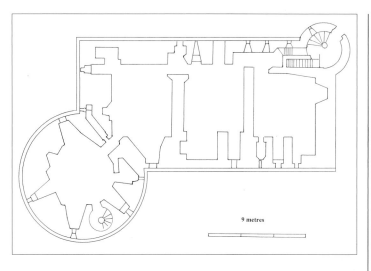

9 metres

Ground-level plan of Huntly Castle; an L2-plan castle dating from 1545 in its present form. The addition of a stair-turret and new entrance in 1602 has caused it to be re-classified in some works as a Z-plan, although the size of the new turret scarcely justifies this. Rather unusually there is a basement floor beneath the ground floor. For the sake of clarity, later additional ranges of buildings to the north-west and east are omitted.

The hall at Doune Castle
The hall or great hall of any castle is usually associated with banqueting, but in most tower houses it was also the place where estate business was conducted. Here at Doune, a game of football is in prospect, once business has been concluded. Note the wooden screen partition, which created a vestibule to serve as a waiting area outside the hall proper.

The castles and tower houses at war

The vast majority of towers might in reality be little more than glorified farm houses, but ultimately they were still expected to be defencible, at least against raiding parties if not armies. Sometimes this was no more than a matter of shutting the door and sitting tight until the raiders had gone, and occasionally enlivening the proceedings by dropping something nasty on anyone getting too close.

If, however, for some reason the attackers genuinely wanted to get in, the focal point was usually the door, hence the early tendency for it to be placed at first-floor level. Walter Scott of Buccleugh, alias 'The Bold Buccleugh', was a notorious exponent of the technique known simply as putting 'fyre to the door'. However this only really worked if the householder had neglected to invest in a yett, which would not only keep any combustibles at a distance but remain secure even if the main door caught light. The standard counter-measure was of course for the defenders to simply pour water over the flames – as Sergeant Molloy did at Ruthven in 1745, when a party of Jacobites tried it – but this depended on there being an internal well or at least sufficient water stored inside. Otherwise it could be dangerous, for, smoke aside, if the fire was allowed to take proper hold there was no way out for anyone inside. In 1630 Viscount Aboyne, John Gordon of Rothiemay and four others died in a mysterious fire at Frendraught, which gave rise to a number of ballads and legends.

More often, the only real chance any attackers had was to take the occupiers by surprise. A not untypical example occurred during an English raid into Dumfriesshire in 1547. Sir Thomas Carleton decided to seize Lochwood Tower, which comprised not only the tower itself but a hall, kitchen and stables, all ringed within a barmekin wall (no doubt exactly as prescribed by the statute of 1535) and surrounded by a moss or marsh. Arriving an hour before dawn, Carleton's men slipped through the moss, and then 12 of them very quietly scaled the wall; they 'stole close into the house within the barnekin, and took the wenches.' At that point they learned there were just two men and another girl in the tower itself, but with no way of getting in all they could do was stay hidden in the house until daylight. Sure enough at dawn one of the men appeared on the wall-head, and seeing all quiet told his girlfriend to open the tower door and rouse the kitchen maids. As she opened the outer door the girl saw Carleton's men, sprang back inside, and very nearly had the door shut again before the raiders burst in and it was all over.

Rather more untypical was the method used by Sir Robert Carey to capture an unnamed Graham peel tower in 1596. It cannot have been a particularly formidable one, for he relates that 'we set presently at worke to get up to the top of the tower and uncover the roofe, and then some 20 … to fall down together, and by that means to win the tower.'

On the whole, and such surprises apart, tower houses were primarily designed to resist bandits and angry neighbours armed with nothing more formidable than muskets, rather than real armies. Instead of attempting to stand a siege against a full-scale invasion it was not

Drochil Castle near Lyne in Peebleshire, engraved by R.W. Billings for the *Baronial and Ecclesiastical Antiquities of Scotland* (1845–52). Although notionally a Z1, Drochil was intended by the Regent Morton to be a palace, and uniquely is designed as a double tenement with a central corridor running the length of the main block on every floor.

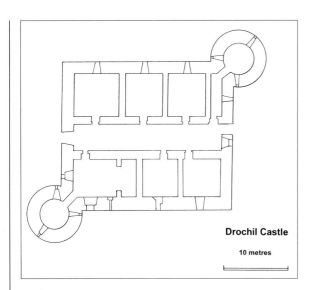

Drochil Castle

10 metres

Drochil Castle, Peebleshire: ground plan. Begun in 1578, work was abandoned after Morton was executed in 1581.

unknown for border peels to be stuffed full of burning peat and then abandoned. Paradoxically enough this generally preserved the structure, for while the internal woodwork might have to be repaired or even renewed, this at least prevented the castle from being demolished by packing the cellars with gunpowder.

The vulnerability of tower houses became all too apparent when they were put to their only real military test in the Great Civil War, which began in Scotland in 1639. The causes and the eventual course of the war are outlined in Campaign 123: *Auldearn 1645*, but for the present purposes it is sufficient to note that whilst most of Scotland rallied behind the National Covenant in opposition to King Charles, there was still substantial support for the Crown in North-East Scotland. Quite apart from the inevitable passage of armies pursuing each other with malicious intent, this resulted in a number of punitive expeditions being despatched to the region and a sorry catalogue of castles plundered unmercifully and occasionally burned, but rarely if ever putting up any kind of defence.

An interesting exception was Gordon of Haddo's house at Kellie in Aberdeenshire (long vanished and replaced by a more conventional country house), and just how exceptional it was may be gauged by this translation from John Spalding's contemporary *Memorialls of the Trubles in Scotland*:

Upon Monday 6th May [1644], the army marched from Udny to the place of Kelly, whereon there was no roof, but the walls strongly standing on the vaults, for the laird [Haddo] dwelt in a 'laigh bigging' [literally a low building or ordinary house, as distinct from a tower] beside it, and had strengthened the walls with soil, whereby men might stand and defend the house.

In other words, in a do-it-yourself attempt to emulate the strengthening of Blackness Castle, Haddo, one of the Royalist leaders, had stripped off the roof, to guard against fire, and piled earth against the inside of the barmekin walls, partly to strengthen them against artillery fire and partly to provide a fire-step for the defenders. Spalding continued:

The Laird had some friends, tenants and servants within the house, well furnished with meat, drink and all other necessary provisions; and a good store of ammunition, such as 'hagbuttis of sound' [probably swivel guns], muskets, carbines, swords, pikes, pistols, powder, ball and such like. [He also] burned up his own stables, barns, byres and other outbuildings lest the same should provide cover for his enemies, and at their approach shot divers 'hagbuttis of sound' and muskets to hold them off.

So far so good. The Marquess of Argyle, representing the government, then equally properly responded by sending forward a trumpeter, 'summoning the Laird of Haddo to render the house, otherwise such as would come willingly out and yield should have conditions of their lives and goods, but they who stood out should have no mercy.' As far as the military etiquette of the day went, this was pretty conventional stuff, but according to Spalding: 'This charge seemed very strange'. Nevertheless it certainly had its effect on the castle's gunner, Walter Richardson, who:

jumped over the wall and stole away to the camp, to the grief of all who were inside. At last the Laird and the rest held a council, where his men

Newark Castle, Port Glasgow, Renfrewshire, as engraved by R.W. Billings for the *Baronial and Ecclesiastical Antiquities of Scotland* (1845–52). This is not to be confused with Newark Castle in Fife, Newark Castle at Ayr, or with Newark Castle near Selkirk.

Terspersie Castle, Aberdeenshire, reconstructed by McGibbon and Ross. A modest but quite classic Z1 tower house built by William Gordon of Lesmoir in about 1561.

declared that they would stick by him, providing he would show them a way to hold out, otherwise they would rather yield now upon conditions, rather than be forced to yield without conditions. The Laird of Haddo was now put to great extremity and could by no means draw them from their opinion, which doubtless was their best, seeing a fearfull [i.e. frightful] army before them and no prospect of relief.

The upshot of course was that they did indeed surrender on Wednesday 8 May, and the plundering then began:

They set in about 36 soldiers to keep the place of Kelly, which they found well furnished with meat and drink, whereon they fed lustily, with about nine score [180] chalders of victual in the girnells, for he had saved much of three years rent and now got nothing for it. Stately was the furnishing within this house with pleasant yards and planting about it. Now the soldiers broke loose and burned most of the tenants houses of Meikle Kelly,

53

Ruthven Barracks 1745

Attacking a tower house could be a frighteningly unsophisticated business, and as late as August 1745 a party of Highlanders tried to capture Ruthven Barracks – a Z-plan structure as it happens – by burning down the back gate. Unfortunately, soldiers firing from the gunloops in the flanking tower shot down one of the men and probably wounded another, after which the fire was extinguished simply by pouring buckets of water over the parapet. Both the attack and defence were absolutely typical of the techniques used for the previous 200 years and more.

Overhill and some of Thornhill, and other building they tore down, took the timbers and made huts with them, and likewise cut down the plantations to be huts and destroyed the hedges. They then slaughtered all the pigs, cattle and sheep, belonging to the Laird on his mains [home farm] and to his tenants wherever they could be found. The Earl Marischal himself took five or six saddle horses of good worth, belonging to the Laird. All of his arms within the house, whereof there were plenty, were plucked up and plundered. There was not one lock, key, door nor window left unbroken down daily to the poor tenants, cottars and grassmen, for fear of their lives had fled here and there through the country from their dwellings, carrying such gear as they could get out of the way. They [the soldiers] broke down beds, panelling, cabinets and other woodwork and burnt the lot.

This sad tale has been quoted at some length by way of emphasising just how indefensible these towers were in real military terms.

Far more typical was an earlier affair at Towie Barclay Castle on 10 May 1639 when a Royalist gang turned up intent on recovering some weapons stored there. However Lord Fraser and the Master of Forbes had word of their coming and 'manned the house of Towie, closed the yetts, and fired divers shots from the house head, whereby a servant of the Laird of Gight's was shot, called David Prat. The Royalists, seeing they could accomplish nothing, left the house thinking there was no point to stay until they too were slain, and so, without more ado rode away.'

Fyvie Castle, Aberdeenshire engraved by R.W. Billings for the *Baronial and Ecclesiastical Antiquities of Scotland* (1845–52). Considerably larger than most and with a history going back to sometime before 1214, Fyvie is nevertheless first and foremost a fortified dwelling house rather than a fortress, built on a somewhat enlarged L-plan.

Ruthven Barracks 1745

The fate of the castles and towers

Naturally enough the fortunes of Scotland's castles were decidedly mixed, but on the whole positive, and most continued in use long after any requirement for 'houses defencible' had faded. The few royal castles of any strategic importance, such as Stirling and Edinburgh, passed into the hands of the British Army. Some lesser castles such as Dumbarton and Blackness continued to be useful despite the decline in their strategic importance: the fact that they could be readily accessed by sea meant they were particularly suitable for stores and ammunition depots. Some, however, such as Ravenscraig in Fife were abandoned to ruin simply because they served no military purpose, while conversely the Jacobite threat gave a new lease of life to others. Inverness Castle was modernised and renamed Fort George to form the third and most northerly of the 'Chain' forts running the length of the Great Glen.

Corgarff, a very plain and undistinguished rectangular tower house in the wilds of upper Strathdon, was taken over by the army and converted into a patrol base. Without that new role it is unlikely that it would have remained in use for long, but instead it has survived and has been fully restored as it was when a lonely detachment of the 13th Foot was based there in the 1750s. The most extraordinary survival of all was Pitreavie Castle, just north of Rosyth in Fife. Originally built as an L-plan tower house by Sir Henry Wardlaw in about 1615, then restored and embellished by its owners in the 19th century, it was

Glenbuchat Castle, Strathdon, by R.W. Billings in *Baronial and Ecclesiastical Antiquities of Scotland* (1845–52). A Z3 completed in 1590.

requisitioned by the Royal Navy in World War II and right up until the end of the 20th century served as a NATO headquarters, thus qualifying as the last of the tower houses to have a 'defencible' function.

Otherwise the survival of castles in private hands depended very much upon their size. Once any military justification for them disappeared, the last of the larger ones, including the remaining enceinte castles, were largely abandoned to ruin, a process that was already well under way by the 16th century. The decline of Urquhart has already been described, and very similarly Kildrummy, having been burned in the aftermath of the Rising of 1715 (it belonged at the time to John, Earl of Mar, the leader of the uprising), was never re-occupied, simply because it was too big, too remote and far too expensive. As the Earl of Strathmore commented in 1677, 'such houses truly are quite out of fashion, as feuds are … the country being generally more civilised than it was of ancient times.'

The smaller castles generally fared rather better, though the smallest such as Evelick were soon abandoned as too cramped and uncomfortable, or at best simply became farmhouses. Those, however, which were at once small enough to be manageable and large enough to be comfortable (which basically ruled out most of the basic rectangular towers) survived as manor houses and country seats, often enlarged and even embellished with additional faux battlements and turrets. Indeed as the wave of romanticism, fostered almost single-handedly by Sir Walter Scott, swept over 19th-century Scotland, a whole architectural style – Scottish Baronial – was inspired by its castles.

Corgarff Castle, Strathdon – the reconstructed barrack room. Note the candle-smoke graffiti on the ceiling, and the equipment hooks. The knapsacks and equipment are based on surviving examples used by the 97th (Invernessshire) Regiment in the 1790s.

Visiting the sites today

Some castles and tower houses, even today, remain in private hands and are often still used as dwelling houses, but those not listed below as 'private' are open to the public. The majority of the surviving examples are, however, in the keeping of one of two organisations: the National Trust for Scotland (NTS) and Historic Scotland. The first is, as its name suggests, a private trust largely dedicated to the preservation of buildings left to it by the original owners and kept in a habitable condition. With few exceptions NTS properties are in the nature of 'stately homes' preserved as when they were last lived in and usually boasting an associated collection of family portraits, furniture and other artefacts presented in their proper and original setting. Historic Scotland on the other hand is a quasi-governmental body (formerly part of the old Department of Works) and looks after a much wider range of properties all the way from the magnificent Edinburgh Castle down to anonymous piles of stone. On the whole, however, it would be fair to say that they tend to be in ruinous condition and some of the smaller and more remote sites are unmanned.

The folowing schedule makes no claim to being comprehensive, but does strive to provide an eclectic selection of those castles particularly worth visiting.

Aberdeen: Provost Skene's House (Aberdeen City Council)

Behind Town House (civic centre) on Broad Street; a fine example of an urban L-plan tower house, currently used as a museum. Within easy walking distance is the old castle hill, largely obliterated by a Salvation Army citadel (in Scottish baronial style) and a tall block of flats. However round the back of both is one remaining bastion of the Cromwellian fort from the 1650s. Also worth viewing is Benholm's Lodging, a Z1 tower house originally situated in the Nether Kirkgate, a street away from Provost Skene's House, but taken down and re-erected stone by stone in Tillydrone Park in the north of the city; it is not open to the public.

Balvenie Castle (Historic Scotland)

Situated at Dufftown in Speyside on the A941, 13 miles west of Huntly (see below) and 17 miles south of Elgin. One of the former Comyn strongholds in an area now considered to be part of the Highlands. Originally a large enceinte castle, it incorporates both an L2 and an L3 tower house.

Blackness Castle (Historic Scotland)

Off the A904 (accessed from Junction 3 on the M9), four miles north-east of Linlithgow on the south shore of the Firth of Forth. The castle itself is just a little way outside the village of the same name, which once served as a port for the nearby burgh of Linlithgow. It features a rectangular tower house within a perimeter wall strengthened for artillery in the mid-16th century. Long used as an ammunition store, it was later rather too enthusiastically pared back to what was understood to be its original condition by the Ministry of Works. The courtyard area, once levelled with earth and gravel, has been scraped down to the living rock.

Bothwell Castle (Historic Scotland)

At Uddingston in Lanarkshire, off the B7071, accessed from Junction 5 on the M74. This is Scotland's largest enceinte castle, dating from the 13th century and featuring a double-towered gateway and an unusual circular keep.

Braemar Castle (private)

Just to the east of the village of Braemar on the A93, 57 miles west of Aberdeen. Situated on what appears to be an early medieval motte, this is a splendid example of an L-plan tower house, which was occupied by the British Army for many years and is surrounded by an interesting loopholed perimeter wall. Within the village of Braemar itself, and very inconspicuously tucked away behind the main street, are the remains of Kindrochit Castle, originally built as a royal hunting lodge in 1371 with square towers at each of its four corners, and rebuilt as a tower house in 1390. Largely robbed out, only fragments of the walling at basement level remain, although it was once the fifth largest tower house in Scotland.

Caerlaverock Castle (Historic Scotland)
Located eight miles south of Dumfries on the B725. An intriguing enceinte castle built on a perfectly symmetrical triangular plan with round towers at two corners and a double-towered gateway at the third. Unusually for Scottish castles it is surrounded by a wet moat.

Castle Campbell (Historic Scotland)
At the head of Dollar Glen, just off the A91, either ten miles east of Stirling or 11 miles west of Junction 6 on the M90 (Kinross Services). This is a rectangular tower, once (obviously enough) in the ownership of the Campbells, and still retaining its barmekin wall.

Castle Fraser (NTS)
Located on a minor road some two miles south of Kemnay, Aberdeenshire. Best approached by way of the A944 from Aberdeen to Dunecht. Probably one of the best surviving examples of a type L2 tower house.

Corgarff Castle (Historic Scotland)
A rectangular tower house occupying a truly desolate setting on the A939 (the Lecht Road) in the hills of upper Strathdon between Cockbridge and Tomintoul. A British officer, Captain Alexander Stewart of Ker's 11th Dragoons, who took part in a raid there in 1746, commented on its remoteness: 'where I dare say never Dragoons were before, nor ever will be again ...' This turned out to be a pretty poor prediction for after the Rising the tower was renovated and turned into a fort with a star-shaped perimeter wall. It has recently been fully restored to its 18th-century appearance.

Craigievar Castle (NTS)
On the A980 about four miles south of Alford, Aberdeenshire. A large and imposing L1 tower house, completed in 1626. Unusually the re-entrant tower is square rather than round and does not house the usual turnpike stair.

Craigmillar Castle (Historic Scotland)
Large medieval castle 2.5 miles south of Edinburgh, just off the A7 by the Royal Infirmary. A courtyard castle with large L-plan tower house.

Crathes Castle (NTS)
Located on the A93 (North Deeside Road) some 14 miles west of Aberdeen, it can also be approached directly from Stonehaven and Dunnottar Castle by way of the famous A857 'Slug Road'. Essentially a rectangular tower house, with a very small jamb that might qualify it as an L-plan. Featuring very elaborate upper works it is chiefly interesting for its internal details including elaborate plaster and tempera ceilings and the woodwork of its top-floor gallery.

Crichton Castle (Historic Scotland)
Located 2.5 miles south-west of Pathhead, off the A68. A courtyard castle originally owned by the Crichtons – who fell from grace shortly after building it.

Dirleton Castle (Historic Scotland)
An unusually tall courtyard castle, in the village of Dirleton, three miles west of North Berwick on the A198.

Doune Castle (Historic Scotland)
Located south of the village of Doune, some eight miles north-west of Stirling on the A84. This imposing courtyard castle was restored in 1883, but happily that restoration was limited to repairing the fabric of the structure and replacing the roof.

Craigston Castle, Aberdeenshire. Remarkably enough this particular house is still in the hands of the Urquhart family, who built it in 1607. This is a fine example of the C-plan – a variant on the more common Z-plan featuring two projecting jambs or wings from adjacent rather than opposed corners – in this case a C2. Although there is corbelling on the outer angles for projecting turrets it does not appear that they were ever built, and similarly what may have been intended as a crenellated wall-head was simply absorbed into the garrets. Another unusual feature is the arch linking the two jambs and supporting a long gallery running across the whole front of the castle. The awkward-looking porch beneath is a later insertion.

Dunnottar Castle (private)

Enjoying one of the most dramatic locations of any Scottish castle, Dunnottar lies on the coast one mile south of Stonehaven, just off the A92, and includes a large L-plan (L0) tower house and a wide range of largely 17th-century domestic buildings, all more or less ruined but largely intact to at least first-floor level. The heavily defended entrance, sporting a quite remarkable collection of gunloops, is particularly interesting.

Edzell Castle (Historic Scotland)

Six miles north of Brechin in Forfarshire on the B966, this is a rich and complex site incorporating a large rectangular tower house dating from the early 16th century, with a later L-shaped range of domestic buildings attached. A pleasaunce or formal garden laid out in 1604 includes a two-storey lodge built in the form of a miniature L2 tower house.

Fyvie Castle (NTS)

Just off the A947 in Aberdeenshire, halfway between Turriff and Old Meldrum. A very imposing L-plan castle with all manner of additions and flourishes, having made the successful translation from tower house to country house. Scene of one of the Marquis of Montrose's battles in 1644, but not actually fought over itself.

Hermitage Castle (Historic Scotland)

A quite awesome – and decidedly eerie – tower-like castle of unique shape, lying between Hawick and Newcastleton in the Scottish borders on the B6399.

Huntingtower (Historic Scotland)

Just west of Perth off the A85 to Crieff, this is an intriguing building originally comprising two quite separate tower houses, linked together in the 17th century.

Huntly Castle (Historic Scotland)

Off the A96 Aberdeen to Inverness road, just on the north side of the town of Huntly. This is a visually impressive ruin, originally known as Strathbogie Castle. Insofar as it can be classified at all, the main block might be considered a large

L2 but it is a very complex site, notable both for the magnificent heraldic entablature above the doorway, which extends most of the way up the stair tower, and for a Civil War earthwork ravelin protecting the unfinished east front.

Kildrummy Castle (Historic Scotland)

Lying ten miles south west of the Civil War battlefield of Alford on the A97. Originally a Comyn stronghold in the hill country of Strathdon, this enceinte castle survived until burnt in the aftermath of the Jacobite rising of 1715.

Linlithgow Palace (Historic Scotland)

In Linlithgow, just off the M9 at Junction 3. Not strictly speaking a castle, but the magnificent ruins of the Stewarts' palace are well worth a minor detour on the way to visiting nearby Blackness Castle.

Lochleven Castle (Historic Scotland)

Chiefly famous for Queen Mary's imprisonment and dramatic escape in 1567, this rectangular tower house is set on an island in Loch Leven, adjacent and just to the east of the M90 – come off at Junction 6 (Kinross Services). The only access is by boat from Kinross, although this is included in the standard admission price.

MacLellan's Castle (Historic Scotland)

Within the burgh of Kirkcudbright on the A711, this is a very rare example of an L4 tower house, in excellent condition.

Neidpath Castle (private)

Rather dramatically set on a steep hillside above the River Tweed, on the A72 just west of Peebles, Neidpath is a well-preserved rectangular tower house.

Newark Castle (Historic Scotland)

On the banks of the Clyde in Port Glasgow, on the A8 at Newark roundabout. This is an interesting example of an L1 in which the original 15th-century tower had a much larger wing added to become the main block.

Provan Hall (NTS)

A good example of an early 17th-century 'laigh bigging' set in Auchinlea Park, Baillieston, Glasgow. It comprises a two-storey main block on an east–west alignment facing a slightly later service block across a small courtyard with the ends closed by walling.

Rothesay Castle (Historic Scotland)

One of the original Stewart castles and built on an extremely unusual circular plan, this 13th-century enceinte castle stands on the Isle of Bute and is accessible by ferry from Wemyss Bay on the A78.

Ruthven Barracks (Historic Scotland)

Just off the A9 at Kingussie. Strictly speaking this is not a castle, but an 18th-century barracks built on the site of Ruthven Castle, another former Comyn stronghold. It is however worth stopping to look at, especially as the Highland Folk Museum is located nearby in Kingussie.

Smailholm Tower (Historic Scotland)

Near Smailholm village, six miles west of the border town of Kelso. A well-preserved but uninhabited rectangular peel tower, still set within the remains of its barmekin wall and in a very remote setting accessed either from the B6397 at Smailholm village or from St Boswell's (on the A68) by the B6404.

Spynie Palace (Historic Scotland)

Some two miles north of Elgin, off the A941. Spynie was the palace of the Bishops of Moray; the main tower, all of six storeys high, was built between 1461 and 1482.

Tantallon Castle (Historic Scotland)

An unusual castle built by the Douglas family, which effectively comprises a large enceinte built across a headland, three miles east of North Berwick on the A198, which in turn can be accessed from the A1 just west of Dunbar.

Threave Castle (Historic Scotland)

Built on an island in the River Dee three miles west of Castle Douglas on the A75. This is a fairly unremarkable tower house in itself, built about 1369, but the castle is chiefly of interest for the artillery wall thrown up around the tower shortly before it was besieged in 1455.

Tolquhon Castle (Historic Scotland)

North of Aberdeen and four miles east of Old Meldrum, this interesting, very late, courtyard castle, incorporating an earlier rectangular tower house, is reached by a minor road off the B999 Aberdeen to Tarves road.

Urquhart Castle (Historic Scotland)

Fully described elsewhere, this magnificent castle, incorporating a rectangular tower house, lies on the western shore of Loch Ness, on the A82 just south of Drumnadrochit. Parking and visitor facilities have been greatly improved in recent years.

Pitrievie Castle near Rosyth began life as a simple L-plan tower house, and was restored and extended in the 19th century. Until recently it served as a NATO headquarters.